A PRAYER MANUAL

BE SURE TO WATCH FOR
NTIAMOAH JAMES KWARTENG'S LATEST
BOOKS:

IS JESUS GOD?

In this great book, James answers questions that have been asked for ages concerning the triune God and the true role of Jesus Christ of Nazareth in the Godhead.

When you have read IS JESUS GOD?, you will have full understanding and be able to explain to those who ask you the same questions you have been asking.

THE RULING GODS ON PLANET EARTH

(Soon To Be Released)

As you read The Ruling Gods On Planet Earth you will receive insight and deliverance. James reveals how cultural beliefs, traditions, and ignorance have us bowing to gods we may not have even heard of. Through gleaning this information, scales will be removed from our eyes, burdens lifted from our shoulders as we walk in the freedom imparted through this must-read book.

To purchase contact:

KINGDOM WARRIORS INTERNATIONAL MINISTRIES, INC.
ntiamoahkwarteng3@gmail.com

A PRAYER MANUAL

PLUGGING INTO GOD FOR SERVICE

Evangelist Ntiamoah James Kwarteng

PLUGGING INTO GOD FOR SERVICE — Protected by United States and International Laws. All rights reserved in cooperation with and compliance to the United States Copyright Act of 1976 as currently revised whereby any reproduction, whether by mechanical, electronic, audio or visual methods is prohibited except by written consent of the publisher. Brief quotes as specified in United States Copyright Act of 1976 as currently revised are excepted.

All emphasis added to Scripture are at the discretion of the author. Evangelist Kwarteng's publishing style capitalizes nouns and pronouns that refer to God, Lord, Holy Spirit, Father, and/or Son. Also note we choose to not capitalize the name satin and/or various related terms signifying his name.

Scripture references were taken from:
The Authorized King James Version of the Bible, Used by permission.
The New King James Version, Copyright © 1979, 1980, 1982, 1984 by Thomas Nelson, Inc. Publishers. Used by permission.
The New American Standard Bible, Copyright © 1960, 1962, 1963, 1968, 1971, 1972, 1973, 1975, 1977, 1995 by the Lockman Foundation. Used by permission www.Lockman.org.

Plugging Into God For Service
First Printing 2006
Second Edition 2013
Printed in the United States

ISBN13: **978-0989473507**
ISBN-10: **0989473503**

ACKNOWLEDGEMENTS

My heartfelt appreciation first goes to the Lord Jesus Christ who has enabled me to put on paper what He laid on my heart for the benefit of His Church.

My sincere gratitude also goes to the following people who have contributed to the publication of this book, and the success of my ministry:

*****

My dear wife, Gloria, who by her prayer support and periodic questioning, as to where I had reached in the writing of the book, encouraged and permitted me to sit up—often too late in the night—in preparation of this work. I cannot overemphasize my appreciation to you, Gloria, for your help in the completion of this book. God richly bless you.

*****

Sister Lillian Denman of Keller, Texas, U.S.A., has served on the boards of Aglow International Area Board for north central Texas as well as the Fort Worth Lighthouse in Fort Worth, Texas. She is currently a Board member of my ministry, Kingdom Warriors International Ministries, also in Fort Worth, Texas. Sister Lillian is a great encouragement to my family, and a faithful contributor to our ministry. Sister Lillian, Gloria and I dearly appreciate you. More healthy years to your life span!

*****

Sister Velma Crow, of Keller, Texas, U.S.A. founder and president of The Ministry Network/Wisdom Merchants, former Aglow board member. She is a woman of God, who by her sensitivity to the Spirit, decided to format and edit this book for me and assist with getting it published. Sister Velma, may the faithful God lavish on you unending surprises.

*****

Apostle Dr. M. K. Ntumy, Chairman of the Church of Pentecost International, whose prayer life and constructive advices have been a source of inspiration to me as I worked under him in Cote d'Ivoire, West Africa. Apostle, you have been a great mentor to me. Your prayer life and mentorship have contributed a lot to the publication of this book. May the eyes of the great God whom you serve faithfully be perpetually upon you.

*****

Elder Emmanuel Boate, my dear father, friend and brother in the Lord, who, having led me to the Lord, practically taught me the essence of prayer and fasting in my initial stages in Him as we stayed together in the same house. Akwasi, I owe you a lot for the publication of this book on prayer. Be proud in Him for the fruit of your labor.

*****

Daddy Darko, C.E.O. of Darko Farms, Dr. Rod Groomer, Director of Missions, Christ For the Nations Institute, Dallas; I do appreciate all of you for the spiritual impact you have made on my life individually, which too, has culminated in the production of this book. May the Great God reward you in return.

Auntie Felicia, Auntie Lizzy, leaders, and all the members of the Aglow International, New York and New Jersey Lighthouses respectively; may the Lord richly bless you for your prayer support in the publication of this prayer handbook. I appreciate all your benevolence toward the ministry. Be Aglow, for Jesus.

*****

I finally want to say a big THANK YOU to all others who in one way or the other labored to the birth of this book..

TABLE OF CONTENTS

FORWARD i

INTRODUCTION ii

Chapter 1   STIRRING UP THE POWER IN YOU 1

Chapter 2   THE ESSENCE OF OBEDIENCE AND BASKING IN HIS PRESENCE 8

Chapter 3   THE FLESH, A SPOILED CHILD 17

Chapter 4   THE ESSENCE OF SIGNS AND WONDERS 24

Chapter 5   GOD'S SECRET WEAPON 30

Chapter 6   THE PRICE FOR SIGNS AND WONDERS 45

Chapter 7   THE SUBMERSIBLES 57

Chapter 8   PRAYING WITH THE UNDERSTANDING 71

Chapter 9   THE MORE EXCELLENT WAY 84

SUMMARY 89

HOW TO ACCEPT CHRIST AS SAVIOR AND LORD 109

About the Author cxi

FOREWORD

I met Ntiamoah James Kwarteng in 2008, at a prophetic meeting I was attending with our mutual friend, Lillian Denman. It was immediately clear that James is a man of prayer and faith with an insatiable appetite for an even deeper relationship with the Lord. I am convinced this man would be willing to lay down his life for the winning of souls.

This kind of love does not come through mere human desire. It can only come by way of constant communion with the Father through yieldedness to Holy Spirit. Our spirit, soul and body must bow to the Spirit of God within who will carry us into the very Throne Room of the living God. As we commune there He will infuse us with the love that held Jesus to the cross, the love that flows from the very heart of God. There in that sacred presence, we are impregnated with the love by which faith works and miracles happen.

This book, <u>Plugging Into God For Service</u>, will inspire you to allow God to become first priority in your life so that you, too, can become a vessel *"fit for the Master's use"* having purged yourself of the wood and clay that prevent such yieldedness. Your life and/or ministry will no longer be stained with the efforts of flesh but will be an out-flowing of the Spirit of God.

It is not a book lifting up Ntiamoah James Kwarteng, though he could share many miracles of deliverances, healing, provision, etc., the Lord has wrought through him. He is careful to give God the glory and to relate experiences from various individuals as the Spirit of God moved through them to perform His will.

As you read this book may the Lord ignite you with the desire for a more complete union with Himself and if you are already aflame, may the wind of the Spirit fan those flames to greater heights as you stretch forth your life in the service of the living God.

Velma Crow,
President / Founder
The Ministry Network/Wisdom Merchants

INTRODUCTION

I find it an obligation as a minister of God, to write this book with the unique intention to motivate and activate my fellow ministers and other serious-minded Christians into getting the Kingdom work done with a minimum of wasted effort; especially in these last days.

I strongly believe that we, the believers of this very dispensation, are the last days' harvesters of the Kingdom of our Lord Jesus Christ. Present events, according to biblical prophecy, confirm clearly that the Lord's coming is very imminent. Every Bible-reading believer bears witness to this fact. The Lord of the harvest therefore expects us, His servants, to put in every possible effort to snatch as many as possible from the fire of hell before His return.

On the other hand, the devil is relentlessly working twenty-four hours a day in order to send the highest possible number of people he can lay hands on to hell-fire. The recent tsunamis that occurred in the Indian peninsula and in Japan, claimed hundreds of thousands of souls instantaneously. There are fires, floodings, tornados, and earthquakes in unprecedented number and severity all over the world. These catastrophic events are vivid proof of how determined the devil is for business. The so-called Islamic Jihad and clashes between rebels and government forces in many countries where atrocities are being carried out every day is also a sure sign of the enemy's determination to populate hell.

May the Spirit of the Lord **in you** grant you understanding as you read this book. May He especially grant you the grace to put into practice what you are about to read so that you can invaluably benefit from it and become one of God's generals in His last day's harvest. May you be a *firebrand* in the hands of the Holy Spirit after reading this book. Amen!

CHAPTER 1
STIRRING UP THE POWER IN YOU

We have been anointed with the <u>same</u> Holy Ghost and power with which the Father anointed Jesus Christ for His service on earth.

The Analogy Of The Electrical Device:
For any electrical or electronic device you purchase from the store to be functional or useful to you, you will need to **inevitably** and **indispensably** plug it into an electrical source. It is purposely made to function that way. There is no other alternative. Yes, no matter how expensive that device might be; or how beautifully or intricately it might be manufactured, ***it remains useless, until you plug it into a power source***.

As servants of the Lord in His service, we will remain useless, and I mean uselessly useless, until we ***incessantly*** plug in to our source of power and information—**GOD**—for the service He has called us into. **THIS IS THE REASON FOR THIS BOOK.**

The Power In You:

Any person who has experienced Pentecost has an immeasurable deposit of Power in them for service; i.e. to set captives free. **"Ye shall receive POWER, (dunamis) after that the Holy Ghost has come upon you**; and ye shall be witnesses unto Me both in Jerusalem, and in all Judea, and in Samaria, and unto the uttermost parts of the earth" (**Acts 1:8**). Brethren, **we have been anointed with the same Holy Ghost and power with which the Father anointed Jesus Christ for His service on earth.** This is clearly stated in **Acts 10:38**, "How God anointed Jesus of Nazareth **with Holy Ghost and with power**; who went about doing good and healing all that were oppressed of the devil; for God was with Him."

However, this great deposit of Holy Ghost power will lie latent and useless until it is **stirred up**. In **2 Timothy, Chapter 1, verse 6-7**, the Apostle Paul had to remind young Timothy that the power he had received through the laying on of his hands, would lie unproductive in him until it was **stirred up** or **fanned into flames.**

What I am trying to convey to you here can be compared to the story of the Pool of Siloam, where a multitude of sick people were lying, desperately waiting for **the stirring** of the water for their healing. The angel stirring the water brought into it a healing virtue, which could unfortunately heal only one person at a time. Thank God, we are blessed to have a whole fountain of living water in us. (Read **John 4:10; 7:38-**

39) We must let it flow to the thirsty world by incessantly stirring it up.

According to Paul, there are three great divine virtues lying latent in every Pentecostal believer, namely; **power, love and sound mind.** These three gifts constitute a spiritual potency, given to the believer purposely for soul winning and the subsequent care they would need. These gifts don't manifest automatically. They need a regular bustle (shaking, excitement) in order to materialize. That is the only way we, and other people for whose sake they are given, can benefit from them. Consequently, Paul thought it essential to remind young Timothy to bring to fruition these three great divine virtues deposited in his inner man, by stirring them up through much time with the Giver.

Amazingly and interestingly, the Lord Jesus Himself, being God in the flesh, and having been mightily anointed with the same Holy Ghost and power, didn't relax and say, "Since I am God in the flesh and having been mightily anointed by My Father, I believe I can go ahead and accomplish My mission without contacting the Father." Instead, He thought it important and inevitable to regularly stir up the dunamis in Himself, by spending days and nights in prayer to His Father. Sometimes He would spend whole nights in sweet communion with the Father. This was how He was able to fulfill His mission here on earth. *"For this purpose, the Son of God was manifested that He might destroy the works of the devil"* **(1 John 3:8).** Beloved, He is our role model. When our Lord Jesus promised in **John 14:12** that, *"he that believes on Me the works that I do shall he do also; and greater works than this shall he do, because*

I go to the Father," it wasn't something automatic. We have to tread the same path that led Him to do those works—the unbroken communion with the Father; then His Spirit in us will cause those greater works to flow through us.

Shake Well Before Use:

Ignorance can be more deadly than aids.

Interestingly, most of the liquid medicines or foods that you buy from the store have this significant piece of instruction written on them, **"shake well before use."** If you really want to enjoy the full dose of that liquid stuff you just purchased from the store, then obey that simple, but meaningful instruction—**'*Shake well before use.*'** For us to shake this world for the Lord Jesus, or turn it upside-down in the manner of the New Testament disciples, we will need to **shake well** the *dunamis* in us through much prayer coupled with periodic fastings just as they did. We will learn more about their manner of service to the Lord and to the perishing in a subsequent chapter.

The Home Deodorizer:

Let me give you another common analogy of the mechanism of this spiritual exercise I am trying to put across to you. Let us take for example this ignorant woman who desires to deodorize her house. She goes to the store and gets herself some P*lug-In Deodorizers*®. She returns home; and instead of plugging them into the electrical source to begin the deodorizing process, she simply deposits them in every corner of all her rooms, waiting for them to freshen the house. You and I know pretty well that this woman would wait in vain for years, wondering why her house is not deodorized.

Why? The reason is quite simple. There is **only one-way** to bring out the sweet aroma enshrined in those little bottles. They are called '*plug-ins.*' Therefore all she needs to do is to unwrap them, fix them, plug them in, and she as well as her visitors can freely enjoy the fragrance. Brethren, ignorance can be more deadly than aids.

Since the birth of the Church on the day of Pentecost, all those who have experienced Pentecost are repositories of the aroma of Christ for this dying world. We must of necessity let it loose for its beneficiaries (i.e. the perishing) by continuously basking in His glorious presence; thus plugging into Him to let loose the saving fragrance of the knowledge of Christ.

The Analogy Of The Magnetic Field And The Pin:

The magnitude of a person's anointing
is determined by the amount of time he spends with
me
in diligent prayer.

Let me share with you a powerful lesson the Lord once taught me about how to get hooked to, and draw power from Him for service. This incident has greatly radicalized my prayer life from that time since. It occurred during my visit to a friend's tailoring shop. On his cutting table sat a small magnet having some safety pins attached to it. Curiously, I was attracted to it. I detached one of the magnetized pins to see if I could pick up a few pins lying idle on the table. Trying to put my little knowledge I have in physics into practice.

With that one magnetized pin, I was able to pick up about four of those idle pins and kept them hanging for a period of time, then they started dropping down. I tried in vain to pick them up again.

All of a sudden, the Lord dropped this formidable truth into my mind. *"James,"* said the Lord, *"I can be likened to this piece of magnetic field, and you, the pin. Just as that one pin was strongly magnetized by exposure to the magnetic field **by reason of the duration of time** it stayed attached to it, so am I able to 'magnetize' or **empower** any servant of mine who develops the invaluable habit of **constantly** staying attached to Me through seasons of prayers.* "You see," He continued, *"the eventual dropping of the picked-up pin, was as a result of the demagnetization of the first pin by which they were sustained.*

"Therefore," said the Lord, "*the only way a pin can **stay** magnetized, and be able to **impart** magnetic force into other unfortunate pins which lack access to the magnetic field, is to **persistently** stay attached to the field.*

"Remember," insisted the Lord, "***the longer** the pin stays attached to the magnetic field, **the stronger** its magnetization. In like-manner, **the magnitude of a person's anointing is determined by the amount of time he spends with Me in diligent prayer.** This is **how** one can hear from Me and draw multitudes to Me.*

*"Again, remember that I am the vine, and you, My servants, are the branches. No branch of mine can **ever** bear fruit without **abiding** in the vine. I have ordained you to go and bear fruit; an abiding fruit. If you want to bear **abiding** fruit for Me, then you will have to **abide in Me through much prayer**. By so doing, you will never lack fruit-bearing as a result; because by your constant communion with Me, I will show you My plans for fruit-bearing. This is the only way I can be glorified through you."*

There is no short cut in this, beloved.

I conclude this part then, by saying that a man's anointing to set captives free, is measured by the amount of time he spends with God in his prayer closet. One person with the Lord can make a great difference. Amen!

QUESTIONS

1. What are the two most significant times in your life that God has been a power source?

2. How have the three great, divine virtues been stirred up in your life?

3. How is Holy Spirit power released in your life?

4. How is prayer likened to a magnetized object?

CHAPTER 2
THE ESSENCE OF OBEDIENCE AND BASKING IN HIS PRESENCE

"They obey Me to the letter. They say and do exactly what I tell them. This is where the secret of their awesome power lies."

The Secret Of Angels' Power:
Once I asked the Lord the following searching question, "Lord, why are angels so much more powerful than us even though, unlike them, we were created in Your own image?" His answer left an indelible mark on my prayer life. *"James,"* the Lord said, *"their secret is twofold. One is because, they are* **always basking** *in My glorious presence, and as a result of My awesome glory covering them, they are rendered invincible. The second is by reason of their* **obedience***. They obey Me to the letter. They say and do exactly what I tell them. This is where the secret of their awesome power lies."* **Awesome!**

Two Typical Examples:
To confirm the above truth, the Lord asked me to read **Exodus 34:28-30,** and **Luke 9:28-29,** respectively.

The above two portions of the Bible constitute a graphic depiction of how magnificently the glory of God covers and empowers any prayerful and obedient child of God, and in consequence, making him a firebrand and greatly useful in the hand of the Lord.

The following two stories are about two kinds of saviors. The first, being Moses whom the Lord sent to redeem His people from the hands of Pharaoh in Egypt. The second is the Lord Jesus Himself. The two of them knew the great importance of obedience and basking in the Father's glorious presence in order to be able to accomplish their respective given goals.

Moses and The Glory:
In **Exodus 34:28-30,** we read: *"So he (Moses) was there with the Lord forty days and forty nights, he neither ate bread nor drank water. And He wrote on the tablets the words of the covenant, the Ten Commandments. Now it was so, when Moses came down from Mount Sinai, and the two tablets of the Testimony were in Moses' hand, when he came down from the mountain **that Moses did not know that the skin of his face shone while he talked with God.** So when Aaron and all the children of Israel saw Moses, behold, the skin of his face shone, **and they were afraid to come near him.**"*

One, Moses' face shone by reason of his **plugging into God** during all those forty days and nights of fasting and communion with Him. Glory covered him so mightily that the very people he was leading had to flee his presence because of this awesome glory of God on his face. In the same manner, devils can't stand the presence of a prayerful saint. They detect him easily from afar because of the radiant glory on him, and therefore make every possible effort to avoid him any time he approaches their abode; even though, he, himself may not be aware of the incident. The reason being that, no force of darkness can stand the glory of God! Remember, Moses had to cover this glory on his face for a longer period of time because the people could not approach him whenever he wanted to convey messages from God to them.

Moses' Obedience:
Now, with respect to obedience, Moses was a role model in every aspect of his walk with the Lord until the unfortunate incident at Kadesh, in the desert of Zin. There, in his anger against the rebellious people, he disobeyed the Lord by hitting the rock twice with his rod, instead of speaking to it as instructed by the Lord. However, the Bible clearly testifies to the faithfulness of Moses in **Hebrews 3, verses 2b and 5**:

"...*as also Moses was faithful in all His house....And Moses verily was faithful (obedient) in all His house, as a servant for a testimony of those things which were to be spoken after.*" He even became a friend of God.

The Lord's Example:
Now listen to this magnificent example of the Lord Jesus, Himself, the second and great Savior, who came to save humanity from the grips of Satan and

his demonic forces. *"Now it came to pass, about eight days after these sayings, that He took Peter, James and John, and went up on the mountain to pray.* **As He prayed,** *the appearance of His face was altered, and His robe became white and glistering"* **(Luke 9: 28-29).** Wow! *"As He prayed."* Not as He slept or watched TV or browsed the internet for Sunday's message (as it is the habit of some); but **as He prayed**! I like that. In fact, this was the Master's life style. His specific and regular hideouts were mostly on the mountains, where He would spend hours praying and hearing from the Father.

During His earthly ministry, it is estimated that He spent two thirds of His time in His Father's presence in order to draw power, hear from Him, see and do what He saw Him do. This daily communion with the Father made His work easier. It was not surprising that He had that irresistible glory of the Father all over Him. He always rendered demons uncomfortable by His glorious presence either in the synagogues or in the public.

Jesus' Obedience:
With respect to the Lord's obedience to His Father, He was perfect. He climaxed His obedience by accepting to die on the cross; and as a result, He was given a name which is above every name, at the mention of which, every knee should bow, and every tongue confess that He, Jesus, is LORD. Amen.

I am convinced that these divine experiences of Moses and our Lord Jesus Christ, due to their regular indulgence in constant communion with the Father, can also happen to us *if only we will learn to discipline our flesh* and diligently seek His face through seasons of prayer and fasting as they both did.

The Invisible Protective Fire:
Flames of fire burn round about a few peculiar people as a protective shield.

Omo Oba Jesu, (*this is the name the Lord gave to him, when He miraculously saved him*) a Nigerian evangelist I met in Suleja, in 1982, who was one time a wizard and a witch doctor said the following about the difference between prayerful and prayer-less Christians.

He said while he was a wizard, he used to see (with his spiritual eyes) two categories of people, both of them wearing the same special white robe, and apparently belonging to one family. However, something peculiar distinguished one group from the other. The first group, which, he said, was very few in number; always had a flame of fire burning in diameters around them wherever they go; even though they themselves do not realize this divine phenomenon. He said no devil, witch or wizard could approach these distinctive people by reason of the fire round about them. They always avoided them whenever they spotted them from afar. Exactly as in the case of Moses when the people avoided him because of God's glory on him. According to him, this strange phenomenon puzzled him all his life in witchcraft until he inquired of the Lord after his conversion, who, precisely, these peculiar people were.

The Lord told him that both groups are His children; and the same white robe that both of them were wearing is called *"the robe of righteousness"* with which He clothes every person who accepts Jesus as his/her Savior. (Read about this robe in **Isaiah 61:10**) "However, those *few peculiar* people who have flames of fire burning round about them as a protective shield are those who have developed the divine habit of spending ***at least*** **two hours a day in prayer,**" said the evangelist. The Lord further told him that, the more a saint prays, the stronger his protection against the enticement of sin becomes, and the easier he is able to bear fruit for Him. Memorize and do **Luke 22:40** as a homework assignment. (Luke 22:40: Pray that ye enter not into temptation.)

Wow, this is a powerful incentive for diligent prayer! The above story also reminds me of a never-to-be-forgotten incident related to me by my father in the Lord concerning a prayerful brother in Ghana named J.C.K., who was at that time a college professor but now a great servant of God. The story was about a Christian sister who had left Ghana for U.K. to continue her university education.

While there, she unfortunately joined herself to a sect and got obsessed by a very stubborn demon and eventually became demented. Because she could no longer continue her studies, she was finally flown back to Ghana in order to find a solution for her problem, but to no avail. I was told she had to be chained because of the magnitude of violence she was causing to herself and others. For months, brethren tried in vain to cast out this demon.

One fateful day, a brother among them remembered a powerful testimony he heard about Brother J.C.K., who had one time commanded his dog, which had been dead for over seven hours, back to life. He therefore suggested that he be called upon to intervene in the precarious situation. They readily sent for him. It is said that, as soon as he entered the house, the demon in the lady yelled, "What do you want here?" Brother J.C.K. straightly ordered the demon to keep its calm and come out of her. Right there, the demon left her and she came to herself for the first time in months. They unbound her; she took her bath and was given something to eat. That was the end of the story. What a demonstration of power.

I remember my spiritual father and I went to this brother to inquire about the secret of the awesome anointing upon his life. His secret, he told us, was **plugging into God.**" Much, much, much time with God in prayer and in the Word," He said. No time for TV and unnecessary conversations. Oh, if brethren would catch the glimpse of this secret, we would affect multitudes of lives for The Master.

Beloved, God is not a respecter of people. If He used, and still uses, Brother J.C.K. to this extent, He will also use you and me in the same manner, provided we will tread the same path he is treading, i.e. basking in His glorious presence.

To Every Full-time Servant Of God:
Quite recently, the Lord spoke to me clearly that just as professionals go about their routinely daily duties **eight hours a day**, working hard to earn their weekly or monthly salaries from their employers, so does He expect every full-time servant of His to do if they expect Him to **guide**, **bless** and **use** them. He said He expects every one of His servants to spend **at least three to five hours daily** with Him in earnest

prayer so they can experience His anointing and irresistible presence with them.

To support this truth, He asked me to read **Luke 6:12**; and it reads: *"Now it came to pass in those days that He (Jesus) went out to **the mountain** to pray, and He continued **all night** praying to God."* He said this was His habit. Notice *"the mountain."* This specificity denotes that that mountain was His habitual hideout. "That is how and why I was able to fulfill My God-given goal on earth," He concluded. Read **1 John 1:8**: *"For this reason, the Son of God came into this world, that He might destroy the works of the devil."* **Hebrews 2:14**: *"In as much as the children have partaken of flesh and blood, He, Himself, likewise shared in the same, that through death, He might destroy him who had the power of death, that is the devil, and release those who through fear of death were all their lifetime subject to bondage."*

Paul was a perfect example of the Lord Jesus. In fact he told the Corinthian Church in **1 Corinthians 11:1**, to imitate him as he imitated Christ. One of the ways he imitated Christ was in the area of prayer. He spent nights and days praying. Read with me **2 Timothy 1:3**: *"I thank God whom I serve with a pure conscience, as my forefathers did, that without ceasing **I remember you in my prayers night and day**."* No wonder God used him so mightily.

In the parable of *the persistent widow*, we have this beautiful promise that those of His elect, who will cry unto Him day and night, backed by faith, will be answered **speedily**. Oh, may He draw us closer to the Throne Room of Grace, so we could find grace to speed up the Great Commission and consequently His second coming. Amen.

QUESTIONS

1. What is the significance of obedience in spiritual warfare?

2. How does your prayer life parallel the prayer life of Jesus?

3. According to the converted wizard, how is the fire of God ignited around us?

4. What are the benefits of the surrounding fire?

5. Name ways you imitate Christ in terms of prayer.

6. How do we "qualify" for the same power Jesus walked in and to do the greater works?

CHAPTER 3
THE FLESH, A SPOILED CHILD

Periodically deprive the flesh of food and sleep and certain comforts of life in order to spend those times plugging into God.

The Flesh, A Spoiled Child:
Any true man of God knows the secret of disciplining his flesh in order to fulfill God's call in his life. The flesh is the number one obstacle to our accessing God's best. It always demands comfort, food (three square meals a day), rest, and sleep.

The flesh hates fasting, vigils, and long prayers. It is the number one disqualifier in our Christian race. When the great apostle Paul realized how harmful and lethal the flesh was to his spiritual service to God, (*"For God is my witness,* **whom I serve with my spirit** *in the gospel of His Son....."* **Rom. 1:9),** he developed a very ruthless attitude towards it so he could fulfill his God-given mission. He relates how he did this in **1 Corinthians, Chapter 9 verse 27:** *"But I discipline my body and bring it into subjection, lest when I have preached to others, I myself should be disqualified."*

Now listen to this. After disciplining and subjecting his rebellious body to his inward man, his flesh eventually became obedient and sober, so much so that, out of that obedience were aprons and handkerchiefs sent to heal and cast out devils from people. *"And God wrought special miracles by the hands of Paul; so that* ***from his body*** *were brought unto the sick handkerchiefs or aprons, and the diseases departed from them, and the evil spirits went out of them"* (**Acts 19:11-12**).

Through prayer and fasting, we permit our inward man where the Holy Spirit inhabits, to exercise control over and utilize the outward man For the Father's glory.

The flesh can become a best companion in our walk with God if we will learn to **discipline** it. All it takes is an aggressive and implacable attitude toward it when it comes to our service to the Lord, and it will in the course of time, become yielded and serviceable to its Maker. Don't be afraid to periodically deprive it of food and sleep and certain comforts of life in order to spend those times plugging into God. It will not die. In the Long run, it will become a helpful friend in its disciplined state.

As it is said in the Scriptures, God is no respecter of people. He will use any dedicated vessel of His. You may be a deacon, deaconess or a member in the local Church. All you need is to find time and *plug in to Him*, always having in mind to glorify Him in soul winning, for we've all been called to go and bear abiding fruit (**John15: 16**). If you do so, He will use you mightily for His kingdom sake. Philip was a deacon of the Church in Jerusalem, but because of his dedication to the service of the Lord, he was so used by the Lord that today, his name figures among the prominent personalities in the Bible. All God is looking for is a dedicated vessel.

Spiritual Covetousness:
The dissatisfaction of one's present state constitutes a springboard that propels him to the next stage.

Let me relate another memorable incident about one of my sons in the Lord, Pastor Gordon Asseh, who now pastors a branch of the Church of God Missions in Nigeria. This was about his uncompromising quest for God's power to see captives set free, and how God fulfilled his heart's desire.

According to him, he was one day in a Church service, where a guest speaker had been invited. He said the man of God ministered under such a tremendous anointing, that many were healed from divers sicknesses and delivered from demonic oppressions.

Provoked by such a graphic demonstration of God's power, right after the service he went to inquire of the man of God about the secret of his awesome anointing. The Pastor didn't hesitate to make the secret known to him. *"The secret is much time with the Lord in fastings and prayers,"* said the man of God. He went home rejoicing, having resolved in his heart to tread the same path of this great man of God, in order to be a recipient of like anointing. I call this *"holy covetousness."* The next day, he shut himself up in his room and said to the Lord, "Lord Jesus, I am neither eating, drinking nor coming out of this room, until you anoint me like that man for your service." Oh, brethren, God greatly delights in such spiritual quests!

He said he was there in the room for three days without food and water, crying earnestly to the Lord for His anointing. On the third day, he said, the glory of the Lord so much filled the room he was in that he fell down to the floor. That was it. He got it! He told me that the next Sunday he preached in his Church, people who had been in the Church with demonic problems and sicknesses were all set free; and everybody was astonished about his awesome anointing. This power is still flowing through him because he has not let go of that divine exercise: fasting and prayer.

You can be the next candidate if you are presently dissatisfied with your service to the Lord just as he was. **The dissatisfaction of one's present state constitutes a springing board that propels him to the next stage.**

I am not implying that you should also fast for three days. Be led by the Holy Spirit as to how long you should wait upon Him for much anointing; being always motivated by the desire to see the oppressed set free. The Bible says we should **covet** spiritual gifts. Covetousness is a sin, but not in the context of spiritual gifts.

1 Corinthians 14:1: "Follow after charity, and desire spiritual [gifts]…" In this scripture the word, "desire," could be translated, "to covet or to be heated or boil with envy."

Humble Yourself:
Don't be jealous when you see God using in a peculiar way a brother or sister in your congregation. Avoid jealousy and pride. Go to him/her and inquire about how they got there. Practice what you hear, and you will get there too.

Hear this. **The anointing has nothing to do with our age in the Lord, or the title we hold.**

I recollect going to the above-mentioned brother, when I heard about the anointing on his life. I wanted him to lay his hands on me and impart into me what he had that I didn't have, even though I had led him to the Lord after my ten years conversion. In fact, he was very reluctant in fulfilling my request, but he finally obeyed and imparted a measure of anointing into me when I **adjured** him in the name of the Lord Jesus to lay his hands on me.

At that time, my wife and I were in Bible School in Nigeria, studying to become missionaries. However, I could not even pray for the healing of someone suffering from headache. I returned from him that day, rejoicing because I knew that I had received a portion of his anointing which I was eager to fan into flames. My first time of casting out a demon successfully from a young lady which culminated in the salvation of a lawyer friend who happened to be there during the incident, was after this memorable impartation.

Brethren, all that he said in his prayer for me during this unforgettable moment is being fulfilled in my ministry today.

Watch out for jealousy and pride, they will deprive you of numerous blessings of the Lord.

However, beloved, I have to be frank with you that I had to wage a relentless battle against pride of mind when I decided to go to him for this impartation. The old serpent questioned several times. "Is it not a shame to go to someone you converted to lay hands on you?" Indeed, the old serpent, knows how to deprive you and me from receiving God's best. Let us not allow him.

The Lord Jesus had to allow John the Baptist to baptize Him in order to fulfill scriptures. Do likewise when you see someone flowing in an anointing greater than what you have. The anointing is distributed for the fulfillment of the Great Commission. It is not about us. It is all about Him.

Timothy got his anointing through impartation by his spiritual father, Paul. In the Old Testament time, God had to anoint seventy elders to bear the burden of the people with Moses, by imparting on them the same anointing, which was upon Moses. That is how it works sometimes. **The most important thing here is the preservation and propagation of the anointing**.

Moses had to rebuke jealous Joshua with the following words, when he asked him to forbid the two young men upon whom the Spirit of prophecy had descended in the camp:

"Are you zealous for my sake? Oh, that all the Lord's people were prophets, and that the Lord would put His Spirit upon them" **(Numbers 11:29).** What a leader Moses was! Oh, God, help us to be imitators of Moses in his humility and selflessness in leadership.

QUESTIONS

1. **Is your flesh a hindrance or help (friend or foe) in your walk with God?**

2. **How does one preserve the anointing?**

3. **Do you see your present circumstance as an observation platform or a springboard to your next season?**

4. **List a time you humbled yourself to receive God's best and state the results.**

CHAPTER 4
THE ESSENCE OF SIGNS AND WONDERS

I believe that the Gospel of our Lord Jesus Christ preached without signs and wonders following, lacks confirmation that we are indeed the Messiah's messengers.

The Essence Of Signs and Wonders:
I am fully and fanatically convinced that the most effectual way of drawing multitudes to Christ in our present technological age is through miracles, signs, and wonders.

Of course, I believe that the greatest miracle on earth is the conversion of the regenerated spirit of man by the Holy Ghost. However, just as bait is used in fishing, so miracles, signs, and wonders in His name, constitute a means by which multitudes are brought to conversion.

I heard that someone asked John Wesley about how he was able to habitually draw crowds. His answer was, *"I set myself on fire, and when the crowd comes to see, they get burnt."*

John the Baptist sent two of his disciples to go and inquire of Jesus if He was the one to come or should they look for another. The Bible says that at that same hour, the Lord had cured many of their infirmities, plagues, and of evil spirits; and many that were blind had received their sight. Now, instead of Jesus specifically declaring to the disciples of John that He was the Messiah to come, He told them this: *"Go your way, and tell John what things ye have seen and heard; how the blind see, the lame walk, the lepers are cleansed, the deaf hear, the dead are raised, and to the poor the gospel is preached."* (**Luke 7:22)**.

The meaning of the Lord's reply to John's envoy was that, **the only way the true Messiah could be recognized was via miracles, signs and wonders wrought through the preaching of the good news.**

I therefore believe that, the Gospel of our Lord Jesus Christ preached *without* signs and wonders following, **lacks confirmation that we are indeed the Messiah's messengers.** This kind of gospel can be likened to a soup without salt. It is insipid. It lacks flavor; and nobody would want to eat that kind of soup, except when the person is sick and has been forbidden to eat anything salty, which is very unpleasant.

In like manner, people are getting fed up with a gospel without confirmation. I notice as I read through the gospels that whenever the people came to Jesus, they came for two things—to *hear* Him, and to be *healed* of their diseases. **Luke 5:15 and 6:17** are typical examples of this.

The Bible affirms the above truth in **(Mark 16:20),** *"And they went forth and preached everywhere, the Lord working with them,* and **confirming the Word with signs following."** The word 'confirm' used here, according to Miriam Webster's Dictionary, means: **to provide witness to the validity of.** Yes, God always validates His Word by signs and wonders whenever it comes **through a clean and a plugged-in vessel.** Amen.

The Old Testament Example Of Signs And Wonders:

In the Old Testament, when God sent Moses to the land of Egypt to redeem His people, He validated His Word in the mouth of His prophet by the mighty signs and wonders He performed through him in that pagan land. That was how the people of the land **saw** the vast difference between the gods of Pharaoh and the great and awesome God of the Hebrew nation.

The Bible declares that a mixed multitude followed the Jewish people when they finally left Egypt. I believe that this mixed multitude mentioned in **Exodus, chapter 12, verse 38**, includes people from Libya, Ethiopia and other neighboring countries who literally saw those unprecedented signs and wonders that the Lord wrought in the land of Egypt. They must have said to themselves, *"Wow! These Jews must be a peculiar people to God; it is worth joining ourselves to them. Who knows, this great God may someday have* mercy on us, and engraft us in to His people so we may together enjoy their inheritance."

Listen to this, *"And I will harden Pharaoh's heart, and multiply My signs and wonders in the land"* (**Exodus 7:3**). To them therefore, those notable signs and wonders performed by the great God of the Jews drew a vast line between the gods of Pharaoh and the Creator of heaven and earth—The I AM—who alone deserves to be worshiped forever. Amen.

In fact, God Himself is characterized by sings and wonders. Wherever He is, signs and wonders abound. The *signs* He performs *point* people to Him, whereas *His wonders cause* people *to wonder* about His Greatness and sovereignty. These two elements draw people massively to Him. His word is impregnated with miracles, signs, and wonders. **It will not return to Him void but will accomplish the purpose for which it is sent.**

<u>**Signs And Wonders In The New Testament**</u>:
In **Acts 4**, when Peter and John healed the lame man at the temple gate, five thousand souls got saved right there as a result. Now listen to the prayer of the disciples for the two apostles, Peter and John, when the religious leaders released them, after threatening and warning them not to speak in that Blessed Name:

"And when they heard that, they lifted up their voice to God with one accord and said, Lord, Thou art God who has made heaven and earth and the sea, and all that is in them. Who by the mouth of Thy servant David has said, why did the heathen rage and the people imagine vain things? The kings of the earth and the rulers were gathered together against the

Lord and against the Christ. For of a truth, against Thy holy Child Jesus, whom Thou hast anointed, both Herod and Pontius Pilate with the gentiles and the people of Israel were gathered together, for to do whatsoever Thy hand and Thy counsel determined before to be done. And now, Lord behold their threatening, **and grant unto Thy servants that with all boldness they may speak Thy word; <u>by stretching forth Thy hand to heal, and that signs and wonders may be done by the name of Thy holy Child Jesus</u>"** (Acts 4:23-31).

Note that the disciples didn't ask for strategic planning skills in order to win their then world for the Lord. Instead they asked that *boldness* be granted them to preach the Word fearlessly; and that *more signs and wonders* be performed through the powerful name of our Lord Jesus Christ, by which five thousand souls have been saved in a day as a result of one notorious miracle. This should be the prayer of the Church today! The time is short, and we want to get as many as possible into the Kingdom. Let me make this clear, that strategic planning is of equal importance in soul winning; for without planning, the anointed man or woman will not go far in their ministry. However, signs and wonders get the job done with a minimum of wasted effort.

Lydda And Saron Turn to The Lord:
In **Acts 9:32-35,** we read of a striking account of the powerful effect that miracles have on evangelism: *"And it came to pass, as Peter passed through all quarters, he came down also to the saints which dwelt at Lydda. And there he found a certain man named Aeneas, who had been bed-ridden for eight years, and was sick of the palsy, (a complete lack of*

movement). And Peter said onto him, Jesus Christ makes you whole: arise and make thy bed; and he arose immediately." Now listen to verse 35. **And all that dwelt at Lydda and Saron saw him, and turned to the Lord."**

All that dwelt at Lydda and Saron got converted. The whole population of a twin city was captured for God because of one miracle. Isn't this amazing? Yes, it is! The apostle Peter through whom this soul-sweeping miracle was performed was a man of prayer and fasting. He was a "plugged-in vessel." Read **Acts 9:43; 10 and 11**.

Right after this single miracle, he went back to his source of power for a refill, for he realized that virtue had gone out of him. This is how every man of God should view himself in terms of ministry. We lose considerable power during ministration, therefore the immediate thing to do is to return to our Source of power for a recharge; and this is done in a hideout via fasting and prayer and serious study of the Word.

This is precisely what Peter did after these two notorious miracles. He went for a refill in the house of one of his good friends, Simon, the tanner. Read Acts 9:43; 10:9-12.

QUESTIONS

1. **What is the greatest miracle on earth?**

2. **How does God validate His Word?**

CHAPTER 5
GOD'S SECRET WEAPON

We ministers are like fuel tankers. We have our unique base for a refill—His Presence.

Fuel Tankers:
Fuel tanker drivers always return to base for a refill after delivery; so they can get ready for the next day supply. We ministers are like fuel tankers. We have our unique base for a refill—**His presence**. If we don't return there, we will be ministering empty; void of power, and we will be wondering why we are not making any impact. We **always** need a refill after ministration so we can continually be a blessing to people. *"They that wait upon the Lord shall **renew** their strength"* (**Is. 40:31**).

Note this: **any person who is greatly used by God has a life characterized by fasting and prayer**. This is their secret. This is how they pay the price for much more anointing. Regularly being in His glorious presence is the answer. *"Who has seen such a thing? Who has heard such things? Shall the earth be made to bring forth in one day? Shall a nation be born at once? For as soon as Zion **travailed**, she brought forth her children"* (**Is. 66:8**).

Travailing prayer makes impossibilities possible. Here is the message the prophet is trying to convey to us. It takes years to build a nation. Yes, of course. Under the same token, the earth needs time to be able to produce fruit. These are undeniable facts. However, what the prophet is saying here is that, impossibilities will become possible if a child of God will **travail** in prayer. Thousands of children can be born to God in a day through a travailing servant of God, a thing, which is impossible for a non-travailing servant of God.

A typical example is what occurred on the day of Pentecost. Three thousand souls were added to the Church after about three hours of intensive, travailing prayer in the Spirit in the upper room.

Production and Multiplication
Come throu spiritual violence.

I was told about an American Baptist missionary who had been in an African country for decades, and had not made the least impact on the people. A young minister later came and started his Church in the same vicinity (not intentionally). Just after one year, his congregation had grown by leaps and bounds. Unlike the old missionary, everybody was surprised about the tangible impact this young man was making on the city. Inquiry revealed that, the difference between the two was their time of communion with the Lord of the harvest. The young man was spending nights and days on his knees; whereas the former was feasting and sleeping.

The *"travailing Zion"* in **Isaiah 66:8**, is the Old Testament version of *"the violent"* in **Matthew 11:12**, who take the kingdom by force. **In God's kingdom principles, production and multiplication come through spiritual violence.**

Praying In Other Tongues:
Let me mention something very significant here about how to adequately and violently travail in prayer so as to set captives free. This is about praying in the Spirit. In fact, I will do every reader of this book a great disservice by not making mention of the critical importance of praying in tongues while treating this wonderful topic on prayer.

I am convinced that right after Pentecost, the devil being very much aware of the great devastation someone praying in tongues does to his kingdom, had an emergency council meeting with all his demonic forces. This meeting was for the purpose strategizing how he could counteract this powerful weapon which the Lord has given to His Church for battle against his evil kingdom. And this, he has done and is still doing, by lying to most Pentecostal believers to pray much with their understanding rather than with their spiritual language, which does a great harm to his diabolic network. *"For we wrestle not against flesh and blood, but against principalities, against powers, against rulers of the darkness of this world, against spiritual wickedness in high places"* (**Eph.6:12**).

This is why there is much controversy about speaking in tongues in the Church more than any other topic in the Bible. If the devil could scrape off the phrase, *'speaking in tongues'* from the Bible, he would have done it before now. I want you to know that the devil doesn't waste his time on things which do no harm to his evil empire. But make no mistake; he will fight tooth and nail against anything, which is lethal to his diabolic kingdom. One of which is speaking in other tongues.

Being aware of this truth about tongues, he has managed to deceive many good men of God into hating anything concerning speaking in tongues. On the other hand, some of those who believe in it have *thought it wise* not to teach about or encourage it at all for the fear that it may cause division in their congregations. Unfortunately, the old serpent is on the winning side in such Churches. No wonder, satanic agents, some of whom unfortunately occupy top positions in these churches, have managed to infiltrate into them.

My principal objective in speaking about this blessed gift at this point is to disillusion you of the lies of the evil one, and at the same time, stir you up into praying in the spirit without ceasing **(Eph. 6:18).** *"Praying always with all prayer and supplication in the Spirit, being watchful to this end with all perseverance and supplication for all the saints." "But you beloved, building yourselves up on your most holy faith, praying in the Holy Spirit"* **(Jude vs. 20)**.

Tongues, A Destructive Weapon:
Among all the weapons the Lord has armed His Church with, (The Word, the Name of Jesus, The

Blood of Jesus, Praise etc.), I believe praying in tongues is the only weapon which one can without interception, launch non-stop for hours against the strongholds of the enemy over nations, cities, towns and villages, and **most especially against the strongholds on the minds of people.**

This great weapon is capable of penetrating *every spiritual bunker* of the enemy, fishing out every hidden demon, and likewise weakening their influence over their victims. In fact, it never misses its target. I call it **"The Holy Ghost Precision Guided Missile."** It is the Holy Spirit only who knows **all** the hideouts, plans, and strategies of the enemy against the Church and the world at large. He therefore uses this *destructive* weapon through the intercessory prayer of the saints to liberate both *lawful* (**Isaiah 49:24**) and *unlawful* captives (**2 Timothy 2:25-26**) of the devil.

I want to share with you a story about a young convert named Joseph and his experience with praying in tongues. The story goes like this:

About three and a half years ago, I met and led a young man from the Volta Region, in Ghana to the Lord. After receiving the baptism of the Holy Ghost by the laying on of my hands, I taught him the great importance of praying with his spiritual language. I would awake him around 2 a.m. every morning to pray.

According to him, he habitually prays from 2 a.m. to 5 a.m. every day. One day I called him from the U.S. to know how he was faring. With so much joy in his voice, he narrated this exciting story to me about the great devastation that, someone praying in tongues, causes in the realm of darkness.

He said after returning from school one day, he heard a knock on his door. When he opened it, to his astonishment, he saw an envoy from his family, consisting of four elderly men who had been sent to him from his home town.

When he inquired (to know) about their mission, they told him that a strange phenomenon, which has never occurred, since the family existed, had taken place in the family home; that the gods of the family are no more responding to their invocations.

In their bid to find a solution the mystery, they went and inquired from a higher hierarchy, a witchdoctor, who eventually revealed to them that he, Joseph, is the cause of the problem. The witchdoctor said that, Joseph's nightly prayers have constituted bombs, which have driven all the gods away from the house. Consequently, the gods claim that, they can no more return there till he stops praying. Wow! What a demonstration of power!

Two months after this formidable demonstration of prayer power, Joseph's aunt, a witchdoctor, being in charge of the family shrine, and who was training fetish priestesses and witches, went personally to the Pastor of the Assembly of God Church, and asked him to come and burn the shrine; claiming that, "If this 24 year old boy has such a power to overthrow our gods, then I want to belong to his God." Praise God.

She is now a born again believer and staunch member of the local Assembly of God Church. Glory to Jesus! Joe believes that gradually, all his family shall turn to Christ by reason of this great miracle.

Interestingly, the distance between Accra, where Joseph lives, and his hometown where the victory occurred is 170 miles. Prayer power knows no limit. Praise God!

If the children of God will pray, we will rule this world and subdue it to Jesus. Especially if we will pray with our spiritual language.

In **2 Timothy 2:25-26**, we read: *"In meekness instructing those that oppose themselves; if God peradventure will give them repentance to the acknowledging of the truth;* **and that they may recover themselves out of the snare of the devil, who has taken them captive to do his will."**

Yes, hearts and minds are liberated in advance from the devil's strongholds of doubt, fear, unbelief, unforgiveness, prejudice, racism, alcoholism, drug addiction, homosexuality, prostitution, witchcraft, false religion, crime etc., and souls are saved in their numbers, when a man or woman of God spends hours upon hours in their prayer closet, bombarding and liberating these captives through his spiritual language **before putting in the sickle**, i.e. **power evangelism,** whereupon signs and wonders become commonplace.

In Pastor Paul Yonggi Cho's message on his prayer life, he relates a chilling story of how through days of fasting and prayer, he managed to battle and defeat a serpent spirit with a human head who had been ruling over the entire population of a country town in South Korea, where he went to evangelize.

According to Pastor Cho, a great revival broke out in that town right after this phenomenal spiritual victory over the ruling spirit. This revival culminated into the miraculous healing of a woman who had been sick and bedridden for seven years, and over whom he had had a challenge from the witchdoctors in that town, who had threatened to kill him and destroy his tent Church if he was unable to raise her up. Praise God, this great man of God knows the secret of bombarding heaven and liberating souls through his spiritual prayer language before putting in the sickle.

There are a lot of ruling spirits influencing entire cities, towns, and villages, whispering diabolic and anti-Christian ideas into the minds of lawmakers who, in turn enact them into laws; thus affecting the free propagation of the blessed gospel of our Lord Jesus Christ. This is why we are admonished by the apostle Paul in **1Timothy, chapter 2, verses 1-2** to intercede *"for kings and all that are in authority that we may lead a quiet and peaceable life in all godliness and honesty."* In other words, through the effectual and fervent prayers of the saints, we are allowing the Holy Spirit to rule over the minds of the lawmakers of our respective nations, imparting into them godly ideas. This is how we, as kings and priests, rule with the Lord Jesus on earth.

Pastor Paul Cho, who now pastors the world's largest church, says in his prayer closet, he spends most of his time praying in his spiritual language. He, just as Smith Wigglesworth and other great men of God, encouraged brethren to pray much in the spirit. As a kingdom warrior, I encourage you as well to use your spiritual language as much as possible for the breaking of strongholds in your home and elsewhere. Pray in tongues while driving, let it flow while in the shower, bombard while doing the washing, and whenever the opportunity presents itself, let these living waters flow from your belly. Launch constantly, these 'Holy Ghost precision-guided missiles,' and expect phenomenal results. Let nobody talk you out of praying in tongues!

The Preciseness of Tongues:
The preciseness of a prayer made in tongues cannot be overemphasized. We read about the preciseness and the effect of intercession made in tongues in **Romans, chapter 8, verse 26:** *"Likewise, the Spirit also helps our infirmities, for we do not know what we should pray for as we ought; but the Spirit Himself makes intercession for us with groanings which cannot be uttered. Now He who searches the hearts knows what the mind of the Spirit is, because He makes intercession for the saints according to the will of God."*

Even though, all the weapons mentioned above, when they are rightly used, have a devastating effect on the arms and plans of the enemy; *"For the weapons of our warfare are not canal, but mighty in God for the pulling down of strongholds...."* (**2 Cor. 10:4**). However, unlike the manner of Jesus during His encounter with the devil, we usually use these great weapons amiss as stated in the preceding verse. On the other hand, the Holy Spirit through our spirits, intercedes (*does warfare*) in tongues on behalf of both the Church and unbelievers alike; thus preventing the enemy to have his way on earth; and under the same token, promoting the Lord's Kingdom on earth.

When Are Battles Really Fought?:
The truth is this, before any physical battle takes place on earth it has already been fought in the spirit realm. Here is a scriptural example: In **1 Kings, Chapter 22**, we read about a battle between Israel and Syria over Ramoth Gilead, a parcel of land belonging to Israel, which Syria had taken through war and how King Ahab decided to take it back.

Now, before Ahab went to battle against Syria over the land, he consulted the four hundred prophets in his palace to know if he could go and win the battle. They all answered him in the affirmative; but King Jehoshaphat of Judah, who had been invited by Ahab to go to battle with him, having discerned the falsehood of their prophesy, requested that another prophet be consulted. When Micaiah, the true prophet of God, was reluctantly called upon by King Ahab, he had this message from the Lord for the two kings, **verse 17.** This verse and other subsequent verses show clearly that that impending battle between the Israeli and Syrian armies over Ramoth Gilead **had already been fought in the spiritual realm.** Then he said, "I *saw* all Israel scattered on the mountains, as sheep that have no shepherd." And the Lord said, "These have no master. Let them return every man to his house in peace."

Ahab hardened his heart and went to the battle in Ramoth Gilead and was killed. The entire army of Israel returned safely in accordance to the vision and the word of Micaiah, the prophet of God.

Beloved, there is a relentless battle going on in the spiritual realm over the souls of men in cities, towns and villages. God is seeking for kingdom warriors who are ready to most times forgo sleep, when He wakes them up in the middle of the night for battle.

This was the secret of the dynamic ministry of our Lord and Savior Jesus Christ. During the night hours, He would go out and spend hours on the mountain alone, battling in intense intercession over the souls of the captives of the enemy and liberate them. He returned in the day time to physically see the multitudes freed from all kinds of ailments by His word. The actual battle and liberation of the multitudes from the enemy's oppression took place during His intercessory prayer in the night. First, comes the spiritual, and then comes the physical.

"Shall the prey be taken from the mighty, or the lawful captive delivered? But thus saith the Lord, even the captives of the mighty shall be taken away and the prey of the terrible shall be delivered; for I will contend with him that contends with thee, and I will save thy children" (**Isaiah 49:24-25**).

In the battle of intercession, we are not alone. The Lord and His host of warring angels always back us. The Church relentlessly interceded for Peter when he was shackled and put in the inner prison. Through their intercessory prayer, an angel of the Lord was sent to release him. Please, join the kingdom warriors now. *"Therefore I exhort first of all that supplications, prayers, intercession and giving of thanks be made for **all men**; for kings and all who are in authority, that we may lead a quiet and peaceable life in all godliness and reverence* (**1Tim. 2:1-2**).

As an intercessor, I advise you to get a map in front of you. Mention countries by name as you pray in your spiritual language beginning with your own country. The Holy Spirit works perfectly through such prayer and dispatches the angels of the Lord to execute the Father's will and purposes on behalf of those countries for which you are interceding. The same thing applies to intercession for individuals. Mention their names as you _bombard_ heaven in tongues for them. Interestingly, as you pray in tongues, the Spirit may sometimes cause you to intercede for an enemy whom you may hesitate to pray for if even prompted by the Spirit to do so.

One of the secrets of the apostle Paul's strong anointing and his effective soul wining was his habit of praying much in tongues. Without hesitation, he declares to the Corinthian Church that he thanks his God that he prays with tongues more than all of them (**1 Corinthians 14:18**). He even goes to the extent of recommending it to all the saints. In **verse 5a, he says, ...I wish that you all speak with tongues...."** Every true warrior or intercessor knows the secret of praying in tongues.

Smith Wigglesworth once said this, that no person baptized in the Holy Ghost should go out from his or her house without first praying in tongues. I recommend then that as an intercessor, you spend most of your time in private praying in your spiritual language.

When I was at Christ For the Nations, the director of my department, Cross-Cultural Missions, Rev. Dr. Groomer who now heads the Missions Department of the Institution—a man I appreciate so much—

recommended that we spend forty-five minutes every morning praying in tongues before classes, thus preparing us for our studies. Isn't it wonderful to have such directors and teachers in a Bible College? Even though I had to travel about forty to forty-five minutes to the campus, I always tried to be there on time in order not to miss that wonderful opportunity. I remember the only times I missed that remarkable occasion was when I missed my bus. As a result of these precious moments spent before classes, out of Dr. Groomer's department have come champions for the Lord. May the Lord of the harvest raise more of such men in our Bible schools to prepare His people to accomplish the Great Commission, especially in these last days.

Sister Sandy, who lives in New York City, is a beloved sister and a family friend. I had the opportunity to preach one Sunday in her local Church. In my preaching, I made mention of the great importance of interceding much in our spiritual language, coupled with regular fastings. The message fell on a good ground; and since then, she has been a firebrand for God. In her ministry, deliverances and different kinds of healings have become commonplace. She loves to spend hours in prayer and the word. She is a Holy Ghost missile launcher. I pray that through the reading of this book, the Lord will raise more of such Holy Ghost missile launchers so we will be able to depopulate hell to populate heaven in the shortest possible time.

The True Story Of A Young Missile Launcher:
To conclude this section, let me relate a true story that a man of God I met in New York about eight

years ago, told me relative to what speaking in tongues does to the kingdom of Satan.

According to him, he was in the living room at a mission house meditating on a scripture he had read, when a young man burdened with the desire to pray popped in and started praying in an unknown tongue at the other corner of the room. He said after a while, he fell into a trance and to his astonishment, saw some missile-like weapons proceeding from that young man's mouth and heading in different directions. The Lord then told him that, that is what happens when one travails in intercession, using his spiritual language.

Demonic networks and influences over nations, cities, towns, and villages are destroyed and evangelism is facilitated in such places. These are places where their heaven is opened. The Holy Ghost missile launchers there have overthrown the ruling demonic forces. Such places become very conducive to evangelism and prayer, miracles abound and souls are easily won for Christ when the word is preached. Places like North Korea, Germany and France, just to mention a few, have their heaven closed because there are not many kingdom warriors there. Islamic nations are also examples of closed heaven. This is the reason God is urging you and me to combat from afar the ruling demons over such nations so that the door for the propagation of the blessed gospel of our Lord Jesus Christ will be opened to them.

QUESTIONS

1. **What makes impossibilities possible?**

2. According to Kingdom principles, how do production and multiplication come forth?

3. Name a time that you know your prayers changed the course of events.

CHAPTER 6
THE PRICE FOR SIGNS AND WONDERS

The only effective way of impacting our present world for Christ will be by signs and wonders done through those who know the secret of plugging into Him.

How Paul Labored:
The great Apostle Paul, who, according to his own account, labored more than all the other apostles through the awesome anointing of God that was on him, said this about the powerful impact that signs and wonders have on evangelism:

"For I will not dare to speak of any of these things which Christ has not wrought by me, **to make the gentiles obedient by word and deed; through mighty signs and wonders, by the power of the Holy Spirit of God**, *so that from Jerusalem and*

round about unto Illyricum, I have fully preached the gospel of Christ." (**Romans 15: 18-19**).

Of a truth, the fame of our Lord Jesus Himself spread so fast due to the unprecedented signs and wonders He did. The same truth applies to Paul. Yes, the only effective way of impacting our present world for Christ will be by signs and wonders done through those who know the secret of plugging into Him.

The Rain Miracle:
Let me relate to you the following true story of the awesome impact that signs and wonders do have on soul wining. This incident occurred in the Ivory Coast, where my wife and I were missionaries for some years. It happened that the leaders of a particular local Church I was working with decided to have a pastoral retreat in a village by the name of Diehiba, situated about seventy miles from the commercial capital city, Abidjan. On Wednesday night during the one-week retreat, the apostle decided that we would have an open-air crusade. Incidentally, I was asked to preach, and my message was titled, "Jesus Is God." A group of villagers gathered to hear the message. When I was done preaching, I threw an invitation for people to accept Christ as their Savior. A few young men and women including some kids raised their hands and came forward. But before I led them to say the sinner's prayer, two of the young men raised their hands up for a question. One of them who assumed the position of a spokesman asked, "Preacher, you just told us that Jesus is God, right?" "Yes," I affirmed. The young man continued. "If Jesus is really God, then we need rains from Him, for we are almost in the fifth month that we've not had rains, and as a consequence, all our rice farms have been destroyed

by the scorching sun; even though we are right in the rainy season."

In fact, my spiritual antennae had been well raised through hours of prayer I had already logged in my prayer closet; and therefore, I was all set to receive from the Lord. Read (Jer. 33:3). Before I could say a word, the Lord told me: "James, tell them that tomorrow I am going to give them torrential rains, and they will continue for a period of three days, and this will be a confirmation to them that I am God." Without hesitation, I conveyed the message to them. I remember hearing someone whispering in French, *"S'il ne pleut pas, on va les chicotte"*—meaning, "If it doesn't rain, we will whip them real good." We said the sinner's prayer and retreated to our various homes.

I quite recollect while going home that night, a pastor friend of mine by the name of Pasteur Abednego, who was my room-mate elbowed me twice, inquiring doubtfully if I really heard the Lord's voice, to whom I answered affirmatively. His fear was somewhat justified because he comes from the *Wobe* tribe, whom we had just evangelized and knew how warlike they are.

At exactly 1:15 a.m. the next day, the Lord Jesus validated His Word, proving to everyone that He is indeed the Living God. A strong wind, which was nearly lifting the corrugated iron roof over the house, started blowing. The torrential rains started pouring; and it poured the whole night and continued for three days as the Lord had said. The Sunday following this miracle saw the Church building filled to capacity. Many were those who were standing outside due to lack of space in the sanctuary. Many people were healed from different kinds of ailments including two mad men.

During testimony time, a young man stood up, but before he could open his mouth, a roar of laughter swept through the place. He quickly reacted to the commotion right after it had subsided, and said, "I know why everybody is laughing. It is because I am a Moslem and a crook. So what is a Moslem doing in a Church? However," he continued, "my testimony is this. I am a rice farmer; and while there was no rain, I prayed five times every day to the god of my religion for rains but to no avail. This preacher (pointing to me) came to preach that Jesus is God.

"No Moslem even believes that Jesus is the Son of God, let alone He being God. I was therefore among the two guys who challenged him for rains from Jesus. Well," he continued, "what I have seen with my naked eyes concerning the torrential rains which poured continuously for three days just as he said, constitute a clear proof to me that Jesus is really God, and as a result, I have decided from this very day to abandon Islam, and dedicate the rest of my life to serve Jesus." **Halleluiah!!**

Another young man who avowed of being almost a wizard, with the sole aim of avenging the blood of his younger sister who, according to him, had been killed by the witches, decided to forgive his enemies and gave his life to Jesus by reason of the rain miracle. The Church, which was composed of only twenty-five members before this remarkable miracle, saw its membership increased to over a hundred and fifty. Glory to the Lord Jesus Christ!

The price for miracles, signs, and wonders is abiding in His glorious presence, which I call Plugging into God.

Yes, Jesus Christ is the same yesterday, today and forever; and He is still confirming His Word by signs and wonders. Amen. However, we need to be in tune to Him to be able to hear Him by spending much time with Him. When we do that, He will instruct us by His Spirit in us.

How Do Signs And Wonders Happen?:
Let me repeat this truth. Miracles, signs, and wonders constitute *spiritual bait* by which multitudes are drawn to God within the shortest possible time.

The ministries of Smith Wigglesworth, Aimee Semple-McPherson, Fuchsia Pickett, John Knox, Katherine Kuhlman, T. L. Osborn, Maria Woodworth-Etter, Benny Hinn, Heidi Bakker, Reinhard Bonnke and Yonggi Cho of Korea, just to mention a few, are examples of what I am trying to carry across to you. I am therefore fully convinced that every **true servant of God** wants to see miracles happen in his or her ministry. Nevertheless, the *inevitable price* to pay for miracles, signs, and wonders, is **abiding in His glorious presence**, which I call **Plugging into God**.

Read the books of any of the above mentioned great men and women of God, as well as any person God has or is using tremendously, and you will bear witness with me that they all talk about the importance of spending *hours* with God before and after ministration in order to draw souls in their numbers to

God. Smith Wigglesworth's ministry was confirmed by great signs and wonders including the restoration of missing limbs. That is how he influenced his then world for God.

Any person who works for God must of necessity, spend much more time with Him than with men. This was the secret of Jesus during His earthly ministry. He was constantly in His Father's presence.

**Do not ignore His presence
for
everything you need for ministry
comes from Him.**

John the Baptist made the following profound statement in **John 3:27** that, *a man can receive nothing, except it be given him from above.* James also said in **James 1:17** that, *"every good gift and every perfect gift is from above and comes down from the Father of lights with whom is no variableness, neither shadow of turning."* It is therefore a dreadful mistake to ignore His presence while working for Him since everything that you will need for the ministry comes from Him.

Whenever you see the anointing waning, go back to Him who is your source of anointing, and **get 'magnetized'**. Preferably, I will even recommend not waiting until the waning of the anointing before getting back to Him; **get inseparably hooked to Him**. Have enough power generated for every situation that will present itself. This is the only way you can effectively work for the Lord of the harvest.

I strongly believe that in these last days, before our Lord's return, there is going to be *a spiritual tsunami* of soul harvesting, which will happen through unprecedented signs and wonders, especially in the Islamic and communist countries. These signs and wonders will be in the form of creative miracles that God, by His infinite wisdom, has purposely reserved for our present dispensation in order to splendidly finalize the harvest.

Since any person who manufactures a device, thinks it wise to make spare parts for replacement in case there is a defect in any of them, I believe that the Source Of Wisdom, the Creator of man, has a storehouse full of human parts awaiting in heaven, *which need to be brought down here* for the restoration of those which have been lost through divers accidents because, they don't belong there in storage. This indeed will be a graphic confirmation of the only blessed gospel of our Lord Jesus Christ, through which multitudes shall be drawn to Him. Amen!

The candidates for this picturesque demonstration of God's power and sovereignty over the works of the enemy shall only be what I call, **"the spiritual submersibles."** Those servants of His who are desirous to *plunge into Him*, ready to ignore most times, their refrigerators, televisions, telephones, the internet and other human contacts *until* they return from on high full of heavenly stuff to glorify Him on earth.

This will be the fulfillment of **Romans 8:18-19** which is the manifestation of **the Children of God** for whom the whole creation is eagerly waiting. Make up your mind to be instrumental in this great harvest! Our Lord's coming is closing in so fast that we should be burdened for the perishing more than ever before.

According to the Apostle Paul in **1 Corinthians 2:10,** there are *deep things of God.* **The anointing to break every yoke of the enemy in people's lives is inclusive.** God also wants us to *hear* from Him and *see* what He does. These are also part of the deep things of God. The Bible calls the above, "word of knowledge" and "word of wisdom." **They are usually and sorely given to those who have their 'spiritual antennae' highly raised for best reception via regular fastings and prayer.**

It is the earnest desire of the Master of the harvest to powerfully anoint us for His service, so we can turn our present world upside down for Him. All He is eagerly waiting for are dedicated men and women who are willing to forgo the comfort of this life and draw closer to Him with the earnest expectation to see captives set free. This is called **passion.** *Passion is what one is willing to suffer and even die for.* He wants to glorify His awesome name through such individuals. Dare to be one!

Launch Into The Deep:
Peter, an old-time fisherman, had toiled all night fishing; and to his surprise did not catch a fish. His encounter with the Master Fisherman dramatically changed his mind-set about *fishing* for good. He alone knows best. Amen.

Let us read the above account in the gospel of **Luke, Chapter 5, and verses 4-6**. *"Now when He had left speaking, He said unto Simon,* **launch into the deep,** *and let down your nets for a catch."* In other words, what the Lord was telling Peter was this: **"There is a place for the draught** that you have been toiling for all night. You haven't been there yet—*that place is in the deep.* Therefore if you want to experience a draught you've never had in your life, simply **obey** My instructions *and launch in to the deep."*

After a little argument with the Lord; *"Master we have toiled all night and caught nothing,"* Peter finally consented to do the Master's bidding by launching into the deep. He eventually experienced one of the greatest miracles which left an indelible mark of faith in his life. **Verse 6** says, *"and when they had done this."* Done what? **Obeyed and Launched into the deep**! *"They caught a great number of fish, and their net was breaking."*

Unfortunately, most of His servants are still fishing in the shallow waters, using their own human skills, and they wonder why they are not having a draught. They mistakenly and ignorantly accuse the people of that particular vicinity of being stubborn, insensitive, or adamant to the preaching of the gospel.

No. The problem is not the people; it is us. It is because we haven't obeyed the Master's bid to launch in to the deep. Launching into the deep demands two things. First, you must kill your own ideology of *fishing*, and adopt that of the Master Fisherman. Second, you must obey His instructions in the face of all odds. Listen to this beloved. When God tells you to jump through a wall, don't tell Him, "But Lord, there is no hole there." Just jump, and there will be a hole for you. He makes a way where there is no way. It is only a question of recognizing and obeying His voice.

Raising Your Spiritual Antennae:
God has given to every believer a spiritual antenna. This antenna must be well raised for a better reception from the Holy Spirit **in** us. This divine antenna is called **intuition**. It is by intuition that we hear from the Lord. It is an integral part of our spirit man where divine truths like, word of knowledge, word of wisdom, and revelation about the things of God and the Word of God are communicated to us.

*"But as it is written, eye has not seen, nor ear heard, neither have entered into the heart of man, the things which God has prepared for them that **love** Him. But God has revealed them to us by His Spirit; for the Spirit searches all things, yea, the deep things of God. For what man knows the things of man, **save the spirit of man which is in him**"* **(1 Corinthians 2:9-11).** This is our intuitive spirit. It causes us to know or discern things about God, man, and situations without conscious reasoning. It is most times impeded by worries of this world. However, **there are three ways to sensitize it** so we can clearly hear from God. They are prayer, fasting, and the meditation of the Word. *"Call unto Me, and I will answer you, and show you great and hidden things which you do not know"* **(Jer. 33:3**). Make the above three things a habit, and the Spirit of God will reveal the mind of God to you concerning every situation you find yourself in, so you can impact your environment for Him.

**Praying much in tongues will activate
all the other gifts in you.**

One time, an elderly woman I respected so much in a branch of a church I was pastoring, twice sent for me to come and pray for her healing, in her house. In fact, both times, I impulsively promised to go, but the Holy Spirit restrained me any time I made an attempt to go. One fateful day, I saw this lady and her son whom she had been sending to ask me to come to their house. Customarily, visitors are always asked about their mission, even if one is conversant with (knowledgeable of) the reason of their arrival. This is culturally related.

After praying and thanking the Lord for their safe arrival, I proceeded to inquire about her mission in coming to me. Well, all was about her physical condition. I was getting ready to lay my hands on her, when the Holy Spirit straightly told me, *"James, do not lay your hands on her, she is a witch, and her aim is to harm you. Confront her, and she will avow."* Oh, how wonderful it is to hear His still small voice.

Without hesitation I told her exactly what the Holy Spirit had revealed to me. She starred at me with surprise for about a minute and a half, and candidly conceded. By virtue of this revelation, some diabolic schemes against the church were exposed and destroyed. However, before then, I had been spending at least three hours straight every day in prayer. This was how my inner man's ear was sharpened to hear distinctly what the Spirit told me about this woman.

The Holy Ghost is still in the business of revealing hidden things to us; but we must allow Him to do so by spending much time in earnest prayer. Praying much in tongues will activate all the other gifts in you.

QUESTIONS

1. **How does one pay the price for signs and wonders in his/her life?**
2. **Name one significant way the Apostle Paul labored among the gentiles.**
3. **What is the only way to prevent the anointing from waning?**
4. **What is passion?**
5. **What are two things that "launching into the deep" demands?**
6. **How do we activate the gifts that have been deposited in us by the Holy Spirit?**

CHAPTER 7
THE SUBMERSIBLES

God is seeking for commandoes
—the violent—
in His earthly army
who will respond to this battle call.

The 'Deep' Of God:
The psalmist has something significant to tell us about what the deep enshrines. Read with me, **Psalm 107:23**:

"*They that go down to the sea in ships, that do business in great waters;* **these see the works of the Lord and His wonders in the deep.**"

The Psalmist says that the works and wonders of the Lord can only be found **in the deep**; but the only people, who are capable of **seeing** these works and wonders, are <u>**those who do business in great waters i.e. in the deep sea**</u>.

The sea is very resourceful. Enshrined in it are huge amounts of oil, uranium, and other rich resources, some of which man has not yet been able to discover. Nevertheless, **those working on the surface of it** are riding ignorantly on these great riches unseen to them. To access them, there is a price to pay. The following are the price payers:

The Submersibles:
About a month ago, I was watching a documentary on the Discovery Channel, where they were talking about '*The Submersibles*' and the incredible discoveries they are now making. I saw an entire lake they have recently discovered right under the sea with its own separate borders. They have also found under the ocean, a spring of water as hot as one hundred and seventy degrees centigrade, where no creature can live except some special worms assigned by the only wise God to live there. I also saw some peculiar creatures and picturesque scenes deep down in the sea which we would never see in our lifetime, had it not been these special people named *'The Submersibles' who are risking* their lives to bring to light these naturally concealed things of God's creation, hidden from all men. By their discoveries, these submersibles are enriching people as well as themselves.

Spiritual Submersibles:
God is seeking for *spiritual submersibles*. Anointing for service is very precious to God; therefore it is not easily accessible. It is a hidden treasure; *and it must be diligently sought for.* Those who seek and find it sacrifice whatever it takes to safeguard it. *"Again the Kingdom of God is like treasure, hidden in a field, which a man found and hid it; and for joy over it, he*

goes and sells all that he has, and buys that field" (**Matt.13: 44**). Wow, he sells **all** that he has and buys that field. Why? Because he **knows** that treasure will sustain him and his family, all their life on earth.

I call this an act of violence. Yes, for the Bible says the Kingdom of God is only for the violent. I believe that all the friends of this man, who heard about this business venture of his, would think he was going crazy. Probably the portion of land he bought from the landlord with all his fortune was not worth the price. However, he alone knew what caused him to act so *foolishly*. He'd got a fortune, which will last him all his lifetime. Someone said, "If you put millions of dollars and the anointing before him, he will choose the anointing." Reason? Because by the anointing God can provide him with millions and millions of dollars.

According to science, things which have not yet been discovered in creation are proportionally far greater than those discovered. Scientists call the undiscovered substance **'*dark matter*'.** Bill Gates, who is one of the richest persons on earth, had to sacrifice his time and money in order to innovate one of the greatest blessing to man in our computer age, **'Microsoft Windows.'** This great innovation was one time part of the *dark matter*. I believe it might have taken him years to philosophize and research to arrive at this great discovery. **Any great invention or discovery is never an overnight thing; it is time consuming**, and much thinking is involved.

Valuable Things:

There is a hidden treasure called

Holy Ghost Power in every person who has tasted Pentecost.

God, in His infinite wisdom has always and carefully hidden things, which are of great value to men. Gold, diamonds, oil, silver, and uranium are among the lot. They are all cautiously and minutely hidden by the great and wise God. To access them, **one has to invest** heavily in money, manpower, and time. Once an individual, a group of people, or a nation is able to pay the said price and access any of the above; they become rich for life, and eventually a blessing to humanity.

There is equally a hidden treasure called '**Holy Ghost power'** in every person who has tasted Pentecost. It is hidden in the inner-man. That power needs to be stirred up as already mentioned in a preceding chapter, through time and effort in order to function. This stirring demands violence—violence to *certain friends*: the telephone, the refrigerator, your own comfort, and the system of this world—so you can seek the face of the Lord in seasons of prayer and fasting. You must persevere until the power of the Holy Ghost begins to flow like liquid through you to set the oppressed free.

For one to be willing to pay such a price, it demands passion for ***the captives.*** We read in a preceding chapter that every person who is not born again, be it a president of a nation, a priest, or a pauper, has been taken captive by the devil to do his (the devil's) will. But the good news about this is in **Isaiah 49:24-25**, KJV:

*"Shall the prey be taken from the mighty (the devil), or **the lawful captive** delivered? But thus says the Lord, **even the captives of the mighty shall be taken away, and the prey of the terrible shall be delivered;** for I will contend with him that contends with you and I will save thy children."*

God is seeking for commandoes—the violent—in His earthly army who will respond to this battle call for the deliverance of the prey of the terrible. Are you one of them?

Rev. Paul Yonggi Cho, while relating his prayer life had this to say about how he battled and still battles the principalities and ruling spirits in Japan in order to liberate multitudes of precious souls in that communist land:

"Whenever I go to Japan," he said, *"I force myself to sit down and pray for **five hours** before mounting the podium."* I call this, 'A- Holy-Spirit-missile-launching.'

Through this man's ministry hundreds of thousands of souls in Japan have been won to the Lord. No wonder he has and is able to maintain the world's largest Church. Moreover, in his country, South Korea, he has the honorable privilege to be consulted by the government for counseling during major decisions. I believe it takes a closer walk with the Source of Wisdom—God, for a person to be propelled to such a paramount position.

In Ivory Coast, a young man whose hands were bound behind him and wearing only shorts, was brought to church by his parents. The Lord whispered to me. "Just bind that demon of madness and command it to leave him." I obeyed and did exactly as I was told. The young man became sane right there; and he and his entire family and all those who followed them to Church turned to the Lord at that same hour. **Hallelujah!**

Praying in tongues is the highway to the deep things of God.

This became possible because, before the incident, I had spent ample time in His presence raising up my spiritual antennae for best reception. I could, therefore, hear Him clearly when He whispered those words to me. Oh, how important it is to hear His voice and obey Him. It makes the work easier.

Now, as I said in the preceding chapter, having bought or picked up this book to read is a clear indication that you desire to be instrumental in the last days' harvest. Please, practice these spiritual principles, and you will be a vessel for noble use. If you will have to regret anything at all, it will only be your past prayerlessness.

I want to encourage every kingdom warrior to pray much in tongues. I have already dedicated a portion of this book explaining why it is important to intercede much in tongues. **I believe that praying in tongues is the high way to the deep things of God.** The answer to mysteries said in tongues to God, is revelations, visions, dreams, understanding of deep things in the Scriptures, and many more. *"Call unto Me, and I will answer thee and show thee great and hidden things which you do not know"* **(Jeremiah 33:3).**

The Lord's Example:
The Lord Jesus Himself served the Father through much prayer. *"Then answered Jesus and said unto them, Verily, verily, I say unto you, the Son can do nothing of Himself, but what He sees the Father do, for whatsoever things He does, this does the Son likewise"* **(John 5:19).** He, the Lord Jesus, clothed with this same flesh like ours, saw the preponderant need of plugging into the Father for power and revelations for service. *"And it came to pass in those days, that He went up to a mountain to pray, **and continued all night in prayer to God**"* **(Luke 6:12).**

If Jesus, being God in the flesh thought it inevitable to plug all night into the Source of power and knowledge so as to receive directives from Him to fulfill His mission on earth, what better thing can you and I do than treading the same path as His? Do you know that as a result of this 'all night' communion on the mountain with His Father, which was His habit, He was able to receive specific instructions from the Father, in terms of the choice of the twelve apostles from the lot, who were to continue His work here on earth after His ascension to the Father. Read **Luke 6 verses 13-16**.

This choice of the twelve apostles from the multitude of disciples was perfectly done, so much so that we didn't even hear the least murmur among the rest about it. Isn't that amazing? I am convinced that this became possible by reason of the fact that the names of all the twelve apostles were given Him by the Father during His all night communion with Him. He simply materialized what He had heard from His Father by calling their names out. *"Call unto Me, and I* will answer thee, and show thee great and mighty or hidden things you do not know"* (**Jeremiah. 33:3**).

Remember, it is the same God who told Cornelius, the centurion *when he was in fasting*, specific things about Peter whom He sent to assist him. He told him the name and surname of Peter, the name of his friend—Simon—Simon's profession, and the location of his house, where Peter was lodging. Brethren, we serve the Omniscient God. If we will diligently seek Him, He will not hide a thing from us, and this will boost up our faith in Him. *"Draw near unto God, and He will draw near unto you"* (**James. 4:8**).

The Young Warrior:
In Ghana, a young girl at the age of sixteen who knew the secret of persistency in prayer, was one day waiting on the Lord, when the Lord communicated to her the name of a lady in Togo, precisely in the city of Lome, who had been married to the devil and whom He wanted to set free and use for His glory. The Lord further gave her the lady's home address and the exact location of her father's store in the Lome market. She traveled down there to Lome, and found the said lady sitting right in front of the store indicated by the Lord. As a result of this revelation, the lady has been delivered and the testimony of her former deep involvement in witchcraft, the exposure of the evil schemes of the demonic world against the Church, which confirms Scriptures, and how she has been miraculously set free by virtue of this sixteen year-old prayer warrior is an eye-opener and prayer-booster to all those who listen to it. God is still in the business of revealing unknown things to those who love His presence.

The second benefit of the Lord's all night communion with the Father was that, He tapped from the Father, incredible "dunamis" to heal the sick, and cast out devils from those tormented by them. **Luke 6, verses 17-19** relate this:

"And He came down with them and stood in the plain, and the company of His disciples, and a great multitude of people out of all Judea and Jerusalem, and from the sea coast of Tyre and Sidon, who came to hear Him and to be healed of their diseases. And they that were vexed with unclean spirits were healed. And the whole multitude sought to touch Him; **for there went virtue (power) out of Him** *and healed them all."* We generate lots of power when we remain in His glorious presence.

Most of God's people complain that they don't hear from God. The reason is that they haven't yet learned the secret of persistent communion with their Father. Their antennae are so low!

Here is how it works:
Take for instance when you are in constant communication with a close friend on the phone. Let's say your friend's name is John, and you are Jimmy. John's voice eventually becomes so familiar to you and vise versa. Just as Jimmy's phone rings, he picks it up and inquires, "Hello?" By simply hearing "Hi" from the other end, Jimmy already knows it is John calling. On the contrary, if that regular communication is cut for some time, it becomes hard to easily recognize each other's voice as it used to be. That is why we are admonished to *"pray without ceasing"* **(2Thess. 5:17; Luke18).**

How Anna, The Prophetess, Served The Lord:

Anna's practical way of **serving** the Lord is worth emulating by **every servant** of God. *"Now there was one Anna, a prophetess, the daughter of Phanuel, of the tribe of Asher. She was of a great age, and had lived with a husband seven years from her virginity; and this woman was a widow of about eighty-four years, who did not depart from the temple,* **but [served] God with fastings and prayers night and day"** (Luke, 2:36-38).

It is recorded that, she was one of the two people who were led by the Holy Spirit to the temple, at the time baby Jesus was brought there to be presented to the Lord. The Bible says in **verse 38**, that she spoke to the people around, some divine truths about the Savior's redemptive work He had come to accomplish on earth. These divine truths flowed spontaneously through her at that moment of need because she had already raised her spiritual antennae for best reception from the Father due to the regular hours she had already logged in her prayer closet.

I think it is worth repeating that, for a child of God to get a clear reception from God about how to walk with and serve Him, he must of necessity raise his spiritual antennae; and this is done uniquely through seasons of prayer and fasting, and the meditation of the Word. There is no short cut in this kind of exercise.

A typical example of what I am trying to put across here is found in the book of **Acts, chapter 13, verses 1-3.** *"Now there was in the church that was at Antioch certain prophets and teachers, as Barnabas and Simeon, that was called Niger, and Lucius of Cyrene, and Manaen, which had been brought up with Herod,* *the Tetrarch, and Saul.* **As they ministered to the Lord and fasted, the Holy Ghost said,** *'Separate unto Me Barnabas and Saul for the work whereunto I have called them.'* **And when they had fasted and prayed**, *and laid their hands on them, they sent them away."*

Even though the Holy Spirit had an urgent work for the two brethren, Saul and Barnabas, to perform in the nations, He waited patiently for the appropriate time when their spiritual antennae had been highly raised for clearer and better reception from Him, *through days of fasting and prayer.* There and then He spoke: *"Separate Me Barnabas and Saul for the work whereunto I have called them."* And they heard Him clearly. Amen. Now, for further instructions from the Holy Spirit as to where they should go, they fasted again before sending them off. And the Bible says in **verse 4**, *"So being sent out by the Holy Spirit, they went down to Seleucia, and from there, they sailed to Cyprus."* Praise God!

Note that these two brethren were very precious to the Church, therefore, they wouldn't have released them on any grounds; except by the intervention of the Holy Ghost. Yes, the Holy Spirit had to be in the equation for their release. This was made possible via prayer and fasting.

Seasons of prayer and fastings, will render our spiritual ears like a powerful microphone to the voice of God, capable of capturing the least whisper He makes. You and I will be able to differentiate between the human voice, the devil's and that of the Holy Spirit. In John's gospel, it is said that His sheep hear His voice, and they will not follow a stranger. This can only happen when the sheep refrains from being wayward (is not rebellious). A sheep that is always close to his shepherd knows his voice.

Revival In The Hotel:
I read about a man of God, who, after a crusade returned to his hotel room. While there, he heard some music from the 1st floor. Glancing through his window he saw a group of people dancing in the bar. His attention was drawn to a particular lady who was dancing all alone. The Holy Spirit told him distinctly to go and dance with her. I believe the immediate thing some of us would do after hearing such a voice, would be to rebuke the demon of immorality or adultery. But the man of God knew beyond every iota of doubt, that it was the Holy Spirit speaking to him, even though he felt uneasy about it, he eventually conceded and went to dance with her.

When he arrived, instead of going ahead to dance with her, he said to the lady, "I came to dance with you but there is one thing I always do before anything." "What do you do?" inquired the lady curiously. Before the woman could realize, the man of God was on his knees, praying in tongues. All of a sudden, the lady fell flat to the floor crying at the top of her voice. All the people in the club who came to witness what was happening to her were also thrown to the floor. The Holy Spirit had taken control of the club.

The story goes like this. The man of God stood up and flipped open his New Testament to **John 3:16**. He preached a short sermon, and right there, everybody got converted to Christ. The end of the story is that the hotel is now turned into a Cathedral. **Praise the Lord!**

Even though what the man of God heard from the Holy Ghost (humanly speaking) sounded silly, yet he knew beyond every shadow of doubt that it was the voice of his Master, because he was in tune to Him. May He create the craving for His presence in us. Amen.

About two months ago, a good friend of mine in Houston, Texas, who is a *prayeraholic,* called me and disclosed to me that the Lord had revealed to him something about a man of God in Ghana, who was indulging in fornication and that he should warn him to refrain from it else the result would be his untimely death. He inquired from me if he should call and tell him right then? I answered in the affirmative. He did so, and the young pastor was astonished as to how he knew about his case. He promised to abstain from his immoral life; but he stopped for a while and went back in to it. Two days after, he called and announced to me the sudden death of the young pastor. But before his untimely death, the pastor had confided in my friend that he had grown weak in prayer and that was why he got entangled in the sin of sexual immorality.

In **Matthew 26:41**, the Lord warned his disciples to *pray* so they might *not fall* into temptation. Meaning, the impending temptation will be revealed to you far ahead via prayer before it materializes. This timely revelation will help you to take every precaution necessary to avoid falling in to it. Indeed, no one will go ahead and fall into a pit that he is already aware of. Instead, he will go around it.

QUESTIONS

1. Who are the "Spiritual Submersibles?"

2. What is the hidden treasure in any person who has tasted Pentecost?

3. Have you experienced finding something worth "everything?"

4. What is the key to continually hearing the voice of the Lord?

CHAPTER 8
PRAYING WITH UNDERSTANDING

God expects us to pray according to His will, not according to our own will.

I have dedicated much time in the preceding chapters to expound on the importance and the great benefit of praying in the Spirit. I, however, deem it right to make mention as well something about praying with the understanding.

In **1 Corinthians 14:14**, the Apostle Paul exhorts the Corinthian believers to pray also with their understanding so that the believers present may understand their prayer and say 'amen' to it. **This scenario is about corporate prayer**. The benefit of praying with one's understanding is that the individual praying as well as those who are listening knows and understands what he/she is saying to God, therefore they are edified.

However, in our prayer with the understanding, the tendency of making many mistakes is high. We mostly tend to be selfish in our petitions. The Apostle Paul confirms this in the book of **Romans 8:26,** *"Likewise the Spirit also helps our infirmities:* **for we know not what we should pray for as we ought;** *but the Spirit Himself makes intercession for us with groanings which cannot be uttered."*

James puts it this way: *"Ye ask, and receive not, because ye ask to consume it upon your lusts"* **(James 4:3)**.

God's Will:

Listen carefully to this. God expects us to pray according to His will, not according to ours. **God's will is His word**. We **must** of necessity have much of His word in us, believe it, and use it in our prayer of intercession and petition. In fact, the only language that God understands, when we go to him in prayer, is His word—the unadulterated Word. Therefore, we are instructed, **"Let the word of Christ dwell in you richly (abundantly)** *in all wisdom; teaching and admonishing one another in psalms, hymns and spiritual songs, singing with grace in your hearts to the Lord"* **(Col. 3:16)**. *"If you abide in Me, and My*

words abide in you, *you shall ask what you will, and it shall be done unto you"* **(John 15:7)**.

God's will, which is His word, eventually becomes our will when we saturate our souls with it by daily studying and meditating upon it. I believe that is why John said *"you shall ask **what you will,** and it shall be done unto you."* **1 John 3:22** says it this way: *"And whatsoever we ask, we receive of him, **because we keep His commandments, and do those things that are pleasing in His sight**."*

Brethren, prayer made according to the Father's will, will never go unanswered. To prove to you this truth, let me walk you through the Bible to see tangible examples of people who prayed according to His will, and how God speedily answered them.

Jacob's Prayer:
Let us begin from the life of Jacob. You may have probably heard the story of Jacob and Esau if you ever passed through Sunday School in your local Church. Jacob had cunningly usurped his elder brother Esau's birthright trough the advice of his mother who had heard about Esau's threats to kill him. Because of his treacherous act toward his brother, Jacob fled to his uncle, Laban, and stayed there for a certain number of years.

Now, on God's instructions, he decided to return to home. Pricked by his conscience about the certain consequence of his malicious act, he resorted in vain to convince his brother through material offerings sent through some of his servants. They, however, returned to him with the terrifying news that his brother was coming to meet him with four hundred strong men. Let us continue the story from **Genesis 32, verses 6-12:**

The messengers returned to Jacob, saying, "We came to your brother, Esau, and he is also coming to meet you, and four hundred men with him." (War. Wasn't it? Yes, it was.) *"Then Jacob was greatly afraid and distressed; and he divided the people that were with him, and the flocks and herds and camels, into two companies.* **And he said, "If Esau comes to the one company and attacks it, then the other company which is left will escape."**

Now, listen to his prayer, which is our subject matter:

"Then Jacob said, "O God of my father Abraham and God of my father Isaac, **the Lord who said to me**, return to your country and to your family, and I will deal well with you: *I am not worthy of the least of all the mercies and of all the truth which you have shown Your servant; I crossed this Jordan with my staff, and now I have become two companies. Deliver me, I pray, from the hand of my brother, from the hand of Esau; for I fear him, lest he come and attack me and the mother with the children.* **For you said,** *I will surely treat you well, and make your descendants as the sand of the sea, which cannot be numbered for multitude."*

Jacob knew the God of his father Abraham, that He

was a God who always stuck to and fulfilled His word. In consequence, **he reminded Him** two times in his prayer concerning His promises to him, which convinced him to return to his kindred. God was then **obligated** (legally bound) to fulfill His promises to Jacob, for His word will never return to Him void. And He did perform those promises.

That same night, God showed him clearly that his prayer **based on His sure promises,** had already been answered, and that the battle had already been fought in the spiritual realm with the victory on his side.

Listen carefully to this. I have said in a preceding chapter that, all physical battles take place in the spirit before they materialize on earth. The report sent to Jacob by his servants, when they returned from Esau was, in a way, a revelation to him that there was an impending battle against him and his family, and that he had to do something about it in order to remedy the situation.

The duty of every Intercessor is to pray, receive revelations from God, and to ward off impending doom through effectual and fervent prayers coupled with regular fastings. This is how spiritual battles are fought and won.

Now, how did God show Jacob that his prayer had been answered? He did this via the night visit He paid him when he was left alone by the ford of Jabbok (**verse 22**).

From **verse 24-28**, we read, "*Then Jacob was left alone and a man wrestled with him until the breaking of the day.* **Now when he saw that He did not prevail against him, He touched the socket of his hip; and the socket of Jacob's hip was out of joint as He wrestled with him. And he said, 'Let me go for the day breaks.' But he said, 'I will not let you go until you bless me.'** *So he said to him, 'what is your name?' He said, 'Jacob.' And he said, 'Your name shall no longer be called Jacob,* **but Israel***; for you have struggled with God and with men, and have prevailed.'"*

"Your name shall no longer be called Jacob, (the supplanter, one who takes the place of another by force or trickery), but **Israel,** (Prince with God or Ruler with God**),** for you have struggled with God and with men, and have prevailed.

Moses' Prayer:

Here is a second example of praying the word and having a rapid answer. Moses was a great intercessor, and really knew how to convince God through His word.

In **Exodus, Chapter 32**, the children of Israel provoked God to anger by making a molded calf as their god to return to Egypt because Moses was not coming quickly from the mountain, according to their timing. God intended to consume them in His wrath, while at the same time promising Moses that He was going to make of him a great nation. Moses, being a selfless leader, resolved to stand in the gap.

God knowing that Moses would inevitably stand in the gap for the sinful people, told him, "Now therefore, **let Me alone,** that My wrath may burn hot against them and I may consume them. And I will make of you a great nation."

"Let me alone" This significant expression of God suggests how much God respects and cannot bypass true intercessors, who intercede according to His will, even when His wrath burns hot against a sinful people.

(**Resuming in verse 11**) *Then Moses pleaded with the Lord His God, and said, "Lord, why does your wrath burn hot against Your people whom You have brought out of the land of Egypt with great power and with a mighty hand? Why should the Egyptians speak, and say, 'He brought them out to harm them, to kill them in the mountains, and to consume them from the face of the earth?' Turn from Your fierce wrath, and relent from this harm to your people. Remember Abraham, Isaac and Israel, your servants,* **to whom You swore by your own self, and said to them**, *'I will multiply your descendants as the stars of heaven; and all this land I have spoken of I give to your descendants, and they shall inherit it forever."*

He was reminding God of what He told his father, Abraham, in **Genesis 13 verse 15**, just as Lot separated himself from him. Was his prayer answered? Yes. Let us see it right in the next verse.

Verse 14, *"So the Lord relented from the harm which He said He would do to His people."*

Remember this. Only one quotation of His word in Moses' prayer was enough to convince God.

Moses' Prayer Once Again:
Let us read one more incident about Moses' prayer by the word, and how God rapidly answered his prayer. In **Numbers, Chapter 14**, from verse **11 to 19**, we read:

*Then the Lord said to Moses, "**How long** will these people reject Me? And **how long** will they not believe me, with all these signs which I have performed among them? I will strike them with a pestilence and disinherit them, and I will make of you a nation greater and mightier than they."*

Now listen to Moses' intercession for the people.

(**Resuming in verse 13**) *And Moses said to the Lord; "Then the Egyptians will hear it, for by your might you brought these people up from among them. And they will tell it to the inhabitants of this land. They have heard that you, Lord, are among these people, that you, Lord, are seen face to face, and your cloud stands above them, and you go before them in a pillar of cloud by day and a pillar of fire by night. Now if you kill these people as one man, then the nations which have heard of Your fame will speak, saying, 'Because the Lord was not able to bring this people to the land which He swore to give them, therefore He killed them* *in the wildernesses.' And now I pray, let the power of my Lord be great,* **just as you have spoken saying**, *'The Lord is longsuffering and abundant in mercy, forgiving iniquity and transgression; but He by no means clears not the guilty, visiting the iniquity of the fathers on the children to the third and fourth generation.' Pardon the iniquity of this people, I pray, according to the greatness of your mercy, just as you have forgiven this people, from Egypt even until now."*

Was his prayer answered? Yes! Right after he had finished. Verse 20 says, *"Then the Lord said I have pardoned* **according to your word**.*"* Let us examine how carefully Moses played his cards in his intercession for the people.

Remember in **verse 11**, the Lord repeated two times, '"**How long? How long**?"

Moses, in reply to God's complaint, said, "But Lord, It has come from your own mouth, that, "The Lord is **longsuffering** and abundant in mercy..." Why then this repetition? I could imagine God saying, "This guy Moses is something else! He truly knows my ways. Yes, if I have indeed said that I am longsuffering, where then does this complaint come from?"

Brethren, if we pray according to His word, which is His will, He will surely answer us.

I therefore exhort you to read the word, meditate, memorize, obey and use it whenever you are praying with your understanding. This is how you shall get your prayer answered.

Personal Prophetic Words:
In addition to praying the written Word it is important that you pray with the prophetic words and promises the Lord has given directly to you. The men and women of the Bible did not have scripture to rely upon as we do. We have the benefit of their relationship with God. However, just as they prayed what they heard God say to them, so must we. This is how we contend for the promises He has made specifically to us. He is no respecter of persons and just as surely as He kept His promises to men and women of old, so will He keep His promises to us. Though the enemy would try to block those promises, if we have truly heard God and remind Him of His promises to us, He will bring it to pass.

In **Isaiah 43:26** we are told, *"Put me in remembrance: let us plead together: declare thou, that thou mayest be justified."*

If we don't contend for the promises in our own lives, many will not come to pass due to the war the devil sets against us. He comes to kill, steal and destroy. Our prophetic words and promises are weapons we use to gain the promised land of our lives. We are to remind the Lord of those things He has spoken to us.

Remember, Christianity is called **"The Great Confession."** We acquire all that the Lord has done for us through the cross by confession. Nothing ever existed in our world without confession. The Creator designed every creature in His holy imagination; however, until He opened His mouth, none of them ever materialized. He spoke the universe into existence. He called those things that were not as though they were and they became!

God is Spirit. We are recreated in His image. We are therefore spirits, living in a *shell* called flesh or body because of the planet on which we have to transit. *'That which is born of flesh is flesh, and that which is born of the spirit is spirit"* (**John 3:6**). Our blessings are therefore spiritual. *"Blessed be the God and Father of our Lord Jesus Christ, who has blessed us with every spiritual blessing in the heavenly places in Christ"* (**Ephesians 1:3**).Some of these blessings, we enjoy without seeing them, because they are purely spiritual. Examples are:

- **The joy of the Lord**
- **The peace of God**
- **The righteousness of the Lord with which we are clothed**
- **Our authority over the devil**
- **The shield of faith**, etc.

Nevertheless, because we have flesh equipped with five senses, we need to feel and see most of them tangibly in order to physically enjoy them. Examples are:
- **Our physical healing**
- **Our financial and material wealth**
- **Our favor with men**
- **The call into the ministry**
- **Signs and wonders following the preaching of the gospel**, etc.

Some of us have received specific promises from Him, either through our intuition, word of knowledge or a prophetic utterance from another saint, as to what He has purported to do **in** or **with** our lives before we exit this earth. We need to continually confess and pray them into being. They are being contended by the enemy. Your incessant confession and prayer will bring birth to them. Don't keep quiet. Let your voice be familiar to God. Materialize your blessings!

Pray With The Understanding.

QUESTIONS

1. How do we pray effectively with our understanding?

2. What is the only language that God understands?

3. What is God's will?

4. How does our will come in alignment with God's will?

5. Where do physical battles begin?

6. How did Moses turn away the wrath of God?

7. Write down and study the prophetic words you have received from the Lord.

8. Pray and do battle (contend) with the prophetic words you have received to bring them to pass in your life.

CHAPTER 9
THE MORE EXCELLENT WAY

*An obedient and prayerful Christian
in the hands of the Lord
is a great threat to the devil's kingdom.*

The More Excellent Way:
To conclude, I want to show you a more excellent way in terms of how to maintain God's perpetual presence with you.

Obedience is the first key to exercising authority. Now concerning obedience, Jesus said this about His walk with the Father in **John's Gospel, chapter 8, verse 29**: *"And He that sent Me is with Me; the Father has not left Me alone, **for I always do those things that are pleasing to Him**.* In **Hebrews 5, verse 7** it is said that, *"…in the days of His (Jesus) flesh, when He had offered up prayers and supplications with strong crying and tears unto Him that was able to save Him from death; **and He was heard in that He feared**."*

Certainly, it is good to be prayerful, but it is best to be obedient, because *"...the effectual fervent prayer of a righteous man avails much"* (**James 5:16b**). Demons fear and tremble before such people (the righteous) because God's perpetual presence is with them. That was the Lord's secret in exercising authority during His earthly ministry; and it should be ours too. *"He who says he abides in Him ought (must) himself also so walk just as He walked"* (**1 John 2:6**).

The seven disobedient sons of Sceva tried to exercise authority over a demon, but it mastered, wounded, and caused them to flee naked. **Make no mistake; demons know if you are living right or not**.

Angels exercise authority from God. They do this by **doing** and **saying** exactly what He tells them; and that is one of the reasons they are so powerful just as the Lord told me.

I want to conclude this section by quoting the Apostle Paul in **2 Corinthians 10, verse 6,** *"And having in a readiness to revenge all disobedience, when your obedience is fulfilled."* An obedient and prayerful Christian in the hands of the Lord is a great threat to the devil's kingdom. Devils readily obey such a person. *"**Submit yourself** therefore to God. Resist the devil, and he will flee from you"* (**James 4:7**).

Hearing from God, **doing and voicing it out** to the hearing of men, *without adding anything to it*, will produce mighty results.

It is said about Ezra, a Levite, one of the Jewish captives who returned to rebuild the ruins of Jerusalem that, *"...Ezra had **prepared his heart** to* *seek the law of the Lord, **and to do it**, and to teach statutes and ordinances in Israel"* **(Ezra; 7:10).** Ezra's attitude toward God's Word is worth emulating. This is why he was able to defy the ambush of armed robbers on the highway to Jerusalem, when he led a convoy carrying a considerable amount of gold for the rebuilding of the temple.

You see brethren, there is always the tendency to look for an immediate opportunity to stand before the congregation and teach a revelation we have received from the Holy Spirit while studying the Bible without first taking the pains to practice it. God cannot confirm such a word. Obedience to the Word first then, power follows when we teach or preach it. Live right and demons, sicknesses, and elements around you will obey you when you command them.

Let us read something from **Jeremiah 23:28-29.** *"The prophet who has a dream let him tell a dream. And he, who has My word, let him speak My word **faithfully** (i.e. without adding anything to it). What is the chaff to wheat? says the Lord. Is not My word like a fire? says the Lord. And like a hammer that breaks the rock in pieces?"*

Adding to His word is an insult and He cannot honor it because it is adulterated. *"For whom God has sent speaks the words of God, for God does not give the Spirit by measure"* **(John 3:34).**

The word of the Lord is never ineffectual when it comes out of a prayerful and obedient servant.

God says, His word will not return to Him void; it will surely perform what He pleases, and prosper in the thing for which He sends it. Amen. **It is as sure as the air we breathe daily.** In fact, there is no word like 'failure' in the vocabulary of God.

Why Demons Resist:
One of the main reasons it takes most believers hours, days and even months to cast out devils is most often because of the disobedience in their own lives. I once heard a demon exposing a besetting sin in the life of a man of God who wanted to cast it out. He eventually agreed that what the demon said about him was true, and asked for prayer. Let us be careful brethren, for a great crowd of witnesses surrounds us. **Obedience is a powerful key to victory in spiritual warfare**. *"Submit yourself therefore to God, resist the devil, and he will flee from you"* (**James 4:7**). Never try to cast out a demon when you have disobedience in your life. It is a dangerous move.

The Lord said boldly to his disciples, *"...the prince of this world is coming, and he has nothing in Me"* (**John 14:30**). That was the main reason demons always trembled before Him.

Make up your mind henceforth, to do what is pleasing to the Lord **always**, and His awesome presence will perpetually be with you.

Make a covenant with your mind, your eyes, your ears and your tongue. Dedicate your whole being to the Lord. Don't allow the devil to have any foothold in your life, and you will be a vessel for noble use.

Never settle for God's *good* or *better*—**get to His best**. Be a violent soul winner for the Master. **Plug into God! Stir up the anointing in YOU**, and take a step of faith, beginning by one-on-one evangelism and experience the magnitude of His saving and healing power deposited **in you**.

QUESTIONS

1. What is the first key to exercise authority?

2. What makes demons resist our command? Support with a scripture.

3. How do you prepare your heart to seek and do the Law of the Lord?

SUMMARY

*While He prayed,
the heaven opened.*

SOME NOTABLE THINGS THAT HAPPEN DURING PRAYER

To summarize this prayer manual, I would like to refresh your memory about some precious things which transpire when the believer prays.

Once again, my objective in doing this is to whet your appetite to loving His sweet and awesome presence, where there is abundant supply of every need a person has.

Admonition To Be Steadfast In Prayer:
In the parable of the persistent widow **(Luke 18)**, the Lord Jesus encourages the believer to be untiring in prayer. **Luke 18:1:** *"And He spoke a parable to them*

that men ought always to pray and not lose heart."

The great Apostle Paul also in his epistles to the Churches mentions four times that the believer should never cease to pray.

- *"Rejoicing in hope, patient in tribulation, continuing steadfastly in prayer"* (**Romans 12:12**).
- *"Praying always with all prayer and supplication in the Spirit, being watchful to this end with all perseverance and supplication for all the saints"* (**Ephesians 6:8**).
- *"Continue earnestly in prayer"* (**Colossians 4:2**).
- *"Pray without ceasing"* (**1 Thessalonians 5:17**).

Now the primary questions we have to ask ourselves are these:
- Why this repetition about unceasing prayer?
- Why not sleep, eat, converse, watch TV, or browse through the internet without ceasing, but why PRAY without ceasing?
- **What does unceasing prayer produce?**

Already, through subsequent chapters of this book, we have learned a lot about prayer products. We nevertheless have some more to learn.

Please do not forget that our subtopic is "**Some Notable Things That Happen During Prayer.**" This means what I am going to say here is not exhaustive.

Feel free to add whatever the Holy Spirit has taught or teaches you hereafter.

Number One Reason:
Here is the number one reason for this repeated exhortation to pray without ceasing:

We read this from the book of **John, Chapter 3, verse 27**, that *"A man can receive nothing, except it be given him from heaven."*

Now we all know very well that the primary medium by which we could reach heaven is through prayer; consequently, the statement of John the Baptist here denotes that without prayer, a man would be as miserable as a pauper on earth.

SOME NOTABLE THINGS

HEAVEN OPENS DURING PRAYER:
Since we've known that whatever we need here on earth comes from heaven, then the next and immediate thing that the believer expects when he goes on his knees is that heaven should open to him. **Persistent prayer is knocking, repeatedly knocking on heaven's door**. It will inevitably be opened to us. "...Knock and it shall be opened to you." "...and to him who knocks, it will be opened" **(Mat. 7:7c and 8c)**

Read with me **Luke 3:21-22:** *"When all the people were being baptized, it came to pass that Jesus also* was baptized, **and while He prayed, the heaven OPENED**, and the Holy Spirit descended in bodily form like a dove upon Him, **and a voice came from heaven** which said, "You are My beloved Son in whom I am well pleased." Hallelujah! Praise be to God!

"While He prayed." Not while He was eating or sleeping, but while He prayed. I like that.

"And the Holy Spirit descended." If this world has ever needed the Holy Spirit's intervention, it is now in our evil age. However, He only intervenes when the Church prays. In **Ezekiel 22:30-31** He is telling us just how important this is. *"And **I sought for a man among them, that should make up the hedge, and stand in the gap before me for the land, that I should not destroy it: but I found none. Therefore have I poured out mine indignation upon them**; I have consumed them with the fire of my wrath: their own way have I recompensed upon their heads, saith the Lord GOD."* The Holy Spirit is counting on us to intervene in the affairs of this dying world. May we be plunged into ceaseless prayer in order to saturate the whole earth with His glorious presence.

The next account is in the book of **Acts, Chapter 10, verses 9-11**: *"The next day, as they went on their journey and drew near the city, **Peter went up on the housetop to pray**, about the sixth hour. Then he became very hungry, but while they made ready, he fell into a trance **and saw heaven opened** and an *object like a great sheet descending to him and let down to the earth."*

God is waiting for never-wearying knockers. Are you one of them?

THE GLORY OF GOD COVERS US:
The number two reason to pray without ceasing is that the glory of the Lord God covers the prayerful saint. This glory on him singles him out in the spirit realm, dispels and causes pandemonium among demons when you approach their abode just as we read from a preceding chapter. No wonder the devil fights prayer more than any other thing.

Let us read this beautiful account in **Exodus 34:28-30:** *"So he was there with the Lord forty days and forty nights; he neither ate bread nor drank water. And he wrote on the tablets the words of the covenant. Now it was so, when Moses came down from mount Sinai and the two tablets of the testimony in Moses' hands, when he came down from the mountain, **that Moses did not know that the skin of his face shone while he talked with Him.**"*

What happened to Moses while he talked with God? **His face began to shine** displaying a physical manifestation of having been in the very presence of God, His glory! Wow! This is a powerful stimulus for unceasing prayer.

Here is the next incident depicting how His glory

covers the prayerful child of God. This occurred to Jesus when He went up on the mountain to pray with Peter, James, and John in **Luke 9:28-29**: *"Now it came to pass about eight days after these sayings, that He took Peter, James and John and went up on the mountain to pray;* ***as He prayed, the appearance of His face altered and His robe became white and glistering.****"*

These two typical examples showing that the covering of God's glory on a prayerful Christian is inescapable and necessary. Remember, the two personalities mentioned here were both 'prayeraholics." As aforementioned, our Lord Jesus spent two thirds of His time in His Father's presence, thus, facilitating His ministry on earth.

On the other hand, Paul would spend days and nights in prayer to God. He was therefore enabled to labor for the Master more than all the other apostles. Let us dare to be there too. Amen.

FOR MINISTERS:
If you ever pay the price as a minister in a local Church, and get there, you will be walking through the pews during service, and demons will begin to scream and come out of their victims without any physical effort, for no demon can stand His glory!

I know this about a pastor friend with the Assembly of God Church in Cote d'Ivoire. He would spend hours daily in his prayer closet and during service, he would simply walk the pews and demons began to cry out and leave their victims without him touching them. What a demonstration of the power in setting captives free!

SETTING PRISONERS FREE:
Every believer is called to wage warfare against the enemy over his own soul and those of the perishing. It is clearly spelled out in **Ephesians, Chapter 6, verse 12,** that, *"we are not contending against flesh and blood, but against principalities, powers, rulers of the darkness of this age, and against spiritual hosts of wickedness in the heavenly places."* We, however, need divine strength to do this warfare satisfactorily.

Uninterrupted prayer is the key to this kind of battle. In **Acts, Chapter 12**, from **verse 1 to 10**, we read of the striking account of how Peter, a prisoner was delivered through an angelic intervention as a result of the unabated intercessory prayer of the Church.

"Peter was therefore kept in prison, **but constant prayer was offered to God for him by the Church***. And when Herod was about to bring him out, that night, Peter was sleeping, bound with two chains between two soldiers; and the guards before the door were keeping the prison. Now behold, an angel of the Lord stood by him, and a light shown in the prison and he struck Peter on the side and raised him up saying, "Arise quickly!"* **And his chains fell off his hands.** *Then the angel said to him, "Gird yourself and tie on your sandals," And so he did and he said to him, "Put*

on your garment and follow me."

So he went out and followed him, and did not know what was done by the angel was real, but thought he was seeing a vision. When they were past the first and the second guard posts, they came to the iron gate that leads to the city, which opened to them of its own accord; and they went out and went down one street, and immediately the angel departed from him."

Oh, if the Church will intercede, the Lord of all flesh and spirit will rule on earth, break every chain and liberate captives.

In Koforidua, a city in Ghana where we held an intensive one week revival with the Presbyterian Church, a young girl in her teens with haggard eyes who was being tormented by the witches, was brought to us to be prayed for. The young men who had been praying in vain for her told us that during one of their deliverance sessions, she vomited a live snake which was killed. We were further told that she had as well vomited some blades. She had fresh incisions on both her cheeks which, according to her, were made in the spirit.

When we started praying for her, she vomited a twisted office pin which we still have in our possession as a proof of her total deliverance. Thank God, she is now totally set free. Glory to Jesus!

Her own story after her deliverance goes like this. "In

my sleep, the witches would come for me and transport me to a deep forest where a group of people all dressed in white had gathered. There, I am put in the middle and a designated person would come and make incisions on both cheeks as well as my legs, probably trying to initiate me into witchcraft without my consent.

"In the morning, I would wake up with blood on both my face and legs. I could not sleep nor concentrate when I studied at school by reason of this oppression. I was desperate, being aware that they would come for me the next night.

"Thanks be to the Lord Jesus who has sent you, His servants, to deliver me from the hands of my assailants."

This was a captive to the devil; and there are similar and worse cases than this all over Africa, India, South America, and in many other places in the world. God is seeking for prayer warriors whom He would send to their rescue. **Dare to be one**.

The grace to intercede is readily available at the Throne of Grace. Enter there with the burden to rescue these wretched souls. He will readily lavish it on you, and you will, in the course of time, see and rejoice over the fruit of your labor. Oh, what a joy to see the oppressed set free!

SENSITIVITY TO THE HOLY SPIRIT:

Most Christians wonder when a brother or a sister relates his experience about how God spoke to them, especially in details. "How did he/she hear that?" They question, "How come I don't hear Him speak to me like they do?"

Well, the answer is clear. Their sensitivity to His voice is as a result of their closeness to Him in ceaseless prayer. I have already given you an example in a previous chapter concerning two good friends on regular telephone communication, whose voices become very discernible or familiar to each other. However, once this constant communication ceases, discerning each other's voice becomes a problem.

The same thing applies to our relationship with the Lord. To be sensitive to His voice through His Spirit in us, it is imperative that we stay in an unbroken communion with Him. In fact, I have come to know by personal experience, that prayer coupled with fasting renders one more receptive to The Master's voice. The Scriptures even confirm this fact.

In the book of **Luke, chapter 2, verses 36-38**, we read about how Anna, the prophetess **served** and became sensitive to things of God. *"Now there was one, Anna, a prophetess, the daughter of Phanuel, of the tribe of Asher. She was of a great age, and had lived with a husband seven years from her virginity; and this woman was a widow of about eighty-four years,* **who did not depart from the temple, but** *served God with fastings and prayers night and day. And coming in that instant, she gave thanks to the Lord, and spoke of Him to all those who looked for redemption in Jerusalem."*

The second case in point is that of the prophets and teachers in the Church at Antioch. *"Now in the church that was at Antioch there were certain prophets and teachers; Barnabas, Simeon who was called Niger, Lucius of Cyrene, Manaen who had been brought up with Herod the tetrarch, and Saul.* **As they ministered to the Lord and fasted, the Holy Spirit said,** *"Now separate to Me Barnabas and Saul for the work to which I have called them"* (**Acts 13:1-2**).

Fasting is humbling the soul and allowing the spirit or the inner man to take preeminence over both the soul and the flesh, thus rendering the spirit sensitive to the promptings of the Holy Spirit.

It is great to serve the Lord this way. This is precisely what Anna, the prophetess as well as the ministers in Antioch did.

Set two to three days aside in the week. Fast, pray much in the Spirit, and stay in the Word. Expect to hear from Him.

DURING DECISION MAKING:
The most important decision ever made on earth was hatched through an all night prayer to God. This was the choice of the twelve apostles who were to

continue the Lord's mission on earth. Had the Lord made the slightest mistake that could have jeopardized His mission for good. Read with me from the book of **Luke, Chapter 6 verse 12**: *"Now it came to pass in those days that He went out to the mountain to pray, and continued all night in prayer to God. And when it was day, He called His disciples to Himself and from them, He chose twelve whom He also named apostles: Simon, Andrew, James and John, Philip, Bartholomew, Matthew, Thomas, James the son of Alphaeus, Simon the zealot, Judas the son of James, and Judas Iscariot, who also became a traitor."*

Many serious and irreparable mistakes have been made by God's people because of our failure to consult Him during decision making. King Jehoshaphat was a man of God's heart; however, he was unwise in his choice of friends and business partners. He narrowly escaped death when he was persuaded by King Ahab, the most wicked king of Israel, to go to war with him in Ramoth Gilead, even though a prophet of God had warned them not to go. When He returned, the Lord sent a prophet and told him this:

"And Jehu the son of Hanani, the seer, went out to meet him and said to King Jehoshaphat, 'Should you help the wicked and love those who hate the Lord? Therefore the wrath of the Lord is upon you'" (**2 Chronicles 19:2**).

The same King Jehoshaphat allied himself with Ahaziah, another wicked king of Israel in a business venture, without contacting God. They made ships to go to Tarshish but because it was not in the plan of God, the Lord destroyed all the Ships.

"But the son of Dodavah of Mareshah prophesied against Jehoshaphat saying, 'Because you allied yourself with Ahaziah, the Lord has destroyed your works or business.' Then the ships were wrecked, so that they were not able to go to Tarshish." **(2 Chronicles 37)** This was a waste of money, time, and energy.

Many serious mistakes have been made by God's present day people as well because of our failure to consult Him during our decision making. In our choice of a marriage partner, a prayer partner, a business venture, a business partner, a trip we want to make, etc. **We must of necessity contact our Source of Life who has our future in His hands.**

"In all your ways acknowledge Him, and He will direct your paths," says the wise preacher **(Proverbs 3:6)**.

POWER IN YOUR WORDS:
In Preaching and Teaching:
The apostle Peter in the day of Pentecost spoke under such a tremendous anointing after about three hours of intensive prayer in the upper room, that the hardened religious leaders, after hearing him, were **cut to the heart**, and we are told 3,000 people got

converted right there:

"Now when they heard this, they were cut to the heart, and said to Peter and the rest of the apostles, 'Men and brethren, what shall we do?'" **(Acts 2:37).**

Words that cut deep into the hearts of one's hearers and affect a transformation within them emanate from much time spent in advance by the speaker in His (God's) presence. In our preaching, teaching, and exhortation, we **must** first edify ourselves in His presence before standing in front of God's people; else, we will do them much more harm than the good we intended to do. Many people get board in their local churches as a result of prayerlessness and lack of serious preparation on the part of the preachers and teachers.

I once heard the following funny story by a preacher. The pastor of a church announced at the end of the Sunday service that all the Board members should meet him at the end of the service. To his surprise, he saw among them a member who was not part of the Board. He then asked him, "Why are you here since you are not on the Board?"

"Oh, I thought you were referring to all the '**bored**' members because I am very bored in this church!"

Yes, this member's frankness to his pastor was a vivid proof of how bored he was in that church.

In **Luke, Chapter 24, verse 32,** we find a typical example of how a prayerful teacher or preacher impacts his hearers. *"And they said to one another, did not our heart burn within us, while He talked with us by the way and while He opened to us the Scriptures?"*

This beautiful account is about our Lord Jesus, Himself, when He confronted the two disciples who were on their way to Emmaus, discussing about their doubt of His post resurrection events reported by Mary and some other women who had been to the tomb to witness His resurrection.

Prayer Power During Demonic Confrontation:
As we go out to witness about our Lord Jesus Christ, there comes some times when we are confronted by an agent of the enemy who might intend to prevent us from delivering the blessed gospel of our Lord to the oppressed. We read about the encounter which Rev. Yonggi Cho of South Korea had with the witchdoctors when he went to the countryside to start a church. In such situations, one should be able to demonstrate divine resilience and power of his God which is above all other powers. However, this can only be possible when one knows how to do battle on his knees. Rev. Yonggi Cho, a man of prayer, fought the battle on his knees and converted an entire town. Praise God!

An unfortunate incident happened in northern Nigeria when the Moslems decided to prevent the Christian minority there from evangelizing their converts. When they persisted in their witnessing the Moslems attacked them with clubs and machetes, killed some and burned their churches. The Christians, on their part, instead of going into fasting and prayer in the manner of the disciples in the time of Herod's persecution of the Church, took to arms and retaliated. Results? There was a massacre of innocent believers.

Prayer is the Key! No power in the heavenly places, neither on earth nor beneath the earth can resist the power of prayer. When believers go on our knees for the sake of the propagation of the gospel, we through this manner, engage the heavenly hosts into battle against principalities, powers, rulers of the darkness of this age, and spiritual host of wickedness in the heavenly places **(Ephesians 6:12).** Even though we don't see them, fierce battles take place in the heavenlies over our cities, towns and villages between these territorial spirits who try to influence our lawmakers into enacting laws that favor the diabolic kingdom of their master, the devil.

It is a sin for believers to slumber in this evil era while we've been armed with such powerful spiritual weapons to pull down the **strongholds** of the enemy.

Spirits and Words:
Listen to this. **Always remember this truth, that it is the spiritual which controls the physical.** God created and controls this physical world through the spirit realm. I believe this knowledge will change your

mind-set about yourself and make you a champion on earth when you grasp it. **You are a spiritual being since your new birth.** *"That which is born of the flesh is flesh and that which is born of the Spirit is spirit"* **(John 3:6). You are armed with spiritual weapons which are propelled through words: CONFESSION AND PRAYER.** Spirits fight with or through words. Spirits act like a computer. They act on what you feed them with, either good or bad. If you shut your mouth, you will be conquered. If you open your mouth through prayer and confession of the Word, you will be a conqueror, for the Holy Spirit needs His sword to be able to fight on your behalf, because, *"the sword of the Spirit is the Word of God"* **(Ephesians 6:17).**

"For though we walk in the flesh we do not war according to the flesh. For the weapons of our warfare are not carnal, but mighty in God for pulling down strongholds, casting down arguments and every high thing which exalts itself against the knowledge of God, bringing every thought into captivity to the obedience of Christ" **(2 Corinthians 10:3-5).**

As soldiers of the Lord, we must always be on the offensive in this perpetual battle between evil and good. Don't keep quiet, else you will be defeated. Have much of the unchanging Word in you. Open your mouth and speak it out through confession and prayer. *"And since we have the same spirit of faith, according to what is written, 'I believed and therefore I spoke,' we also believe and therefore speak"* **(2 Corinthians 4:13).**

The more words you feed the Holy Ghost with through much prayer and confession of the creative Word, the greater your victory in this battle. For, *"This is the word of the Lord to Zerubbabel* (also to you and me)*: Not by might nor by power, but by My Spirit, says the Lord of host"* **(Zechariah 4:6).**

HOW TO MAKE TIME FOR PRAYER

The Practicals:

Many believers complain of not having enough time to pray for at least one hour which is the minimum time the Lord has given to His saints to pray. I believe and know this alibi is not true. How do I know this? I came to this tangible conclusion through my visits to some Christian homes as a minister of God. Most times, as I have aforementioned, people spend almost all their time watching television. Some thereby receiving visitors they have no business entertaining. While others while away precious times arguing over politics and other unimportant things. They even sometimes end up fighting over words and break up without prayer. One time, a concerned brother complained to me about his wife spending hours on the phone with an unbelieving friend. What a waste of time!

Since we are told to redeem the time because the days are evil, here are some practical suggestions which will help you utilize your time wisely and find time to pray:

1. Now that you know the value of prayer, **desire to pray.**

2. **Avoid unnecessary conversations**, either on the phone or one-on-one.

3. **Avoid eating** food with carbohydrate contents before going to bed.

4. **Control the television.** I think the most important thing about the TV is to listen to the news or listen to some edifying messages on the Christian channels. Sometimes there are certain important documentaries you may want to hear. Please value the presence of God more than anything else on earth.

5. Be careful **not to be addicted to browsing the internet.** It will eat up your time.

6. **Find time to sleep early** so you can wake up in the night to pray. Spend **at least** one hour praying every night. Time yourself. It is not unspiritual. One hour a night will help build you up spiritually to withstand temptations. *"Then He came to the disciples and found them sleeping, and He said to Peter, 'What? Could you not watch with Me one hour? Watch and pray, lest you enter into temptation. The spirit indeed is willing, but the flesh is weak"* **(Matthew 26: 40-41).**

7. Before you go to bed, **ask Holy Spirit to awaken you** by giving Him a specific time. He is very punctual! Remember that tares are sown during the night time when people sleep. Moreover, there is less distractions during the night time.

8. During rest after prayer, expect God to reveal to you great and hidden things of which you are ignorant. *"Call unto Me, and I will answer you and show you great and hidden things you do not know"* **(Jeremiah 33:3).** Put a pen and paper beside your bed. **Write down and date what the Holy Spirit reveals to you.** Writing is very important to God.

9. **Make sure that you don't fall back asleep when He awakens you.** If that continues for two or three times, He may not wake you up again. The Holy Ghost is a gentleman, and He wouldn't want to bother you when He notices that you love your sleep more than you love Him.

After prayer, get into the Word and study it with interest. Expect God to speak to you as well through His Word as you meditate on His Word. I pray that the Lord grant you grace to do it. Amen.

Pray without ceasing!

May the grace and peace of our Lord Jesus be with you. Amen.

QUESTIONS

1. **How has this book impacted your prayer life?**

2. **Memorize at least one scripture every day.**

I encourage you to reread this book until the Holy Spirit creates in you the irresistible craving for prayer. **Be a firebrand for Jesus!!!**

HOW TO ACCEPT CHRIST AS SAVIOR AND LORD

You may have read this book with keen interest, ready to become a prayer warrior. However, this book is all about **how** to lead people to Christ. Therefore if you have not yet personally accepted Jesus as your Savior and Lord, you may wonder why your prayer goes unanswered. The reason is that the Bible clearly says in the gospel of **John, Chapter 9, verse 31**, that God does not hear the prayer of a sinner. *"Now we know that God does not hear sinners, but if anyone is a worshipper of God and does His will, He hears him."* For you therefore to be heard by God, you will first need to accept Jesus Christ as your personal Savior and Lord. Here is how you can accept Him into your life:

Dear Father, I acknowledge that I am a sinner; and that Your Son, Christ Jesus, came in the flesh, died on the cross and shed His blood for my sins. Please forgive me my sins. I open my heart to you, Lord Jesus; come into my life. I accept You as my personal Savior and Lord. I confess that you are Lord, and that the Father has raised You from the dead. Thank You, Lord, for saving me today. In Jesus' name I pray. Amen.

If you have said this prayer, bear witness of the fact that you are saved and now a part of the family of God by telling someone of this great news. You can notify us at:

Kingdom Warriors International Ministries, Inc.
45 Apple Street
East Legon
Accra
Ghana, W. Africa
ntiamoahkwarteng3@gmail.com
We would love to celebrate your new birth with you.

ABOUT THE AUTHOR

Evangelist Ntiamoah. James Kwarteng originates from the West African country of Ghana. He is a graduate from the Christian Missionary Foundation Institute in Ibadan, Nigeria, and Christ For the Nations Institute of Dallas, Texas, U.S.A., respectively, where he studied Cross-Cultural Missions. James majored in English and French at the Institute of Languages, Kumasi, Ghana. He also learned Spanish from the University of Texas in Arlington, Texas, U.S.A., increasing his language base, knowing that God has called him into a global Ministry.

James and his wife, Gloria were missionaries to Cote d'Ivorie (Ivory Coast), for over a period of ten years, where God tremendously used them for the salvation, healing, and deliverance of many. James has also ministered in other West African nations including, Togo, Burkina Faso, Nigeria, Guinea and Ghana. He is also a minister of note in churches in various states of the United States of America.

Though James and Gloria are both citizens of the United States of America, they have received and responded to the call to return to Ghana as Missionaries, where they began their global ministry, **Kingdom Warriors International Ministries, Inc.** They are blessed with a son and three grandsons.

James primarily teaches and conducts Spiritual Warfare though he is known as an evangelistic deliverance minister. He also teaches Cross-Cultural Missions, Deliverance, and Power Evangelism. His contact information is:

Kingdom Warriors International Ministries, Inc.
45 Apple Street
East Legon
Accra
Ghana, W. Africa
ntiamoahkwarteng3@gmail.com

www.ingramcontent.com/pod-product-compliance
Lightning Source LLC
Chambersburg PA
CBHW061446040426
42450CB00007B/1239